Me

Once

as it was

A Memoir

Griselda Jackson Ohannessian

A New Directions Book

ACKNOWLEDGMENTS

The author wishes to particularly thank Priscilla Baker who, after reading a first chapter, encouraged me to keep on writing; and my sister Kathie, whose typing, editorial suggestions, and enthusiasm spurred me on. She also drew the map of the farm.

The frontispiece photo and the one of The Ruin were taken by John Garber, c. 1938-39. The cover illustration is a detail from an oil painting by Harry Leith-Ross dated 1937 and titled Kit's Skating Party.

Manufactured in the United States of America.
New Directions Books are printed on acid-free paper.
First published by William L. Bauhan, Publisher in 2002, and as a New Directions Paperbook (NDP1054) in 2007.
Published simultaneously in Canada by Penguin Books Canada Limited.

Library of Congress Cataloging-in-Publication Data

Ohannessian, Griselda Jackson, 1927-
Once : as it was : a memoir / Griselda Jackson Ohannessian.
    p. cm.
"A New Directions book."
Originally published: Dublin, N.H. : William L. Bauhan, c2001.
ISBN-13: 978-0-8112-1660-9 (alk. paper)
ISBN-10: 0-8112-1660-8 (alk. paper)
1. Ohannessian, Griselda Jackson, 1927---Childhood and youth. 2. Graves, Robert, 1895-1985--Friends and associates. 3. Jackson, Laura (Riding), 1901-1991--Friends and associates. 4. Bucks County (Pa.)--Biography. I. Title.
   CT275.O44A3 2007
   974.8'21043092--dc22
   [B]

                2006034480

New Directions Books are published for James Laughlin
by New Directions Publishing Corporation
80 Eighth Avenue, New York, NY 10011

This account is for my three daughters who used to ask me to tell them about the "olden days"—my childhood in the 1930s.

And it is for "the kids" as I used to call my two sisters and brother—Maria, Kathie, and Ben—who share many of the same memories.

CONTENTS

Once

as it was

FIRST OFF

Of all my far-back memories two remain most vivid, as if they had just happened. The first is of an incident that occurred in a few minutes' time; the second, a matter of months. The first happening surely was the key to my survival of the second.

The first: I was three and a half years old, it was summer, August 18, 1930, the day my sister Maria was born. Someone must have been watching over me but I don't remember anyone else being there. I do remember clearly the dark red hollyhocks standing against the white wall of the house and I remember knowing that in a room on the floor above me something was happening, a baby was coming. It was a very warm, bright day. Above, the sky completely blue; in the air, a sweet grass smell and the churr of some summer insects. I was looking out on a wide expanse—the lawn, the wooded hillside across the dirt road, the barns, the fields. And suddenly I was filled with a clear sense of myself standing on the earth, the world, a part of all I surveyed yet distinctly me, my self. I knew I was myself and, at the same time, one with the great world turning beneath my feet (it definitely felt rounded) and soaring within the great sweeping sky, an endless yet friendly blue bowl.

The second: I am twelve and a bit, new people have come to stay on our farm. That is a news item in my magazine, *The Jackson Quarterly*: "The old ruin across the road which is on the

3

jacksons' Farm has been rebuilt to a lovely little stone house in which shall live Miss Laura Riding, Mr. Robert Graves, Mr. David Reeves, Mr. Alan Hodge and Mrs. Bearal Hodge. All famous writers from England." "Famous" is a bit of editorial hyperbole but indeed Laura Riding and Robert Graves were well known—and still are—in literary circles; she, especially for her poetry; he, then, for *I, Claudius* and his autobiographical *Good bye to all That*. It was fitting to list Laura Riding's name first, for it was readily apparent that she was the one in command. There is no editorial comment that things were off kilter and odd. There is no hint that something dangerous was in the air when, in fact, there was.

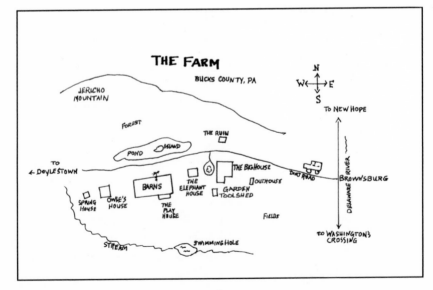

THE FARM

The farm we—my two sisters, my brother, and I—called home was in Bucks County, Pennsylvania. A few years ago, when I last drove by, I saw that the place as we had known it was no longer there. Only vestiges remained. The Big House, as we called it, looks more elegant than it did years ago; fresh white paint, blue instead of dark green shutters, landscape-designer plantings, lawn a brighter, lusher green mowed now with a power mower, not the old hand-propelled one that took the better part of a day to cover all the grassy areas. The trees still stand in stately pairs on the front lawn, site of many games—croquet, baseball, tag, take-a-giant-step, blindman's bluff. Flocks of migrating grackles would noisily descend on these trees in the spring. I can see my father, sometimes in pajamas, dashing out with his shotgun and murderously blasting away. He was an excellent marksman. I think, too, of dried locust shells and acorns. The tree where the orioles nested every year and where we could swing almost as high as the sky still stands in the driveway circle by the side of the house, but it has a tired look. The barns are unused, all but the stone one beginning to fall apart, the barnyard a tangle of weeds. The stone house across the way, built in connection with the troubled times, is no longer visible. The woods have grown up and now hide it from view. The pond it once looked down on has reverted to marshland. The walnut trees, some three hundred of them that threaded the sweep of fields, are gone, uprooted immediately after my mother moved away in 1950. Now much of the land is to become a golf course. Perhaps it already has.

Sixty or so years ago, when the farm was our home, one could drive through it on a dirt lane leading from the River Road, (along the Delaware north to New Hope, south to Washington's Crossing) to another macadam road (west to Doylestown, the county seat). One would not have been particularly struck by the place's appearance. It was not overall a pretty or handsome place, and certainly not elegant. The charm lay in its details—some of them pretty, some handsome, some odd, some hidden from view, all together unique.

The northerly side of the dirt road that ran through the property was mostly woodland sloping up toward the crest of a grandly named hill, Jericho Mountain. The spring that supplied our delicious running water was located in these woods. It was covered with a large board lid, but one could nonetheless still hear its faint gurgle. The ground around it was soggy and the air there seemed to be especially sweet. Turtles and frogs were drawn to this place.

We tramped around these woodlands often. They held all sorts of differing places: ferny spots, mossy areas, stretches where lumbering had left great tree stumps, a fall walk destination when a lone persimmon tree at the top of "our mountain" was ready with its small, puckery fruits, a site where old bedsprings and various other ungainly trash were gradually being covered with vines. Deer lived in these woods and we always hoped to come across them. We never did see them there, but occasionally in the early evening a herd would cross the road below the Cherokee Indians, the Owl's, house to graze in the fields and drink from the brook. Every year a few hunters, regulars, came in the hunting season and left with a deer strapped on the roof of their car and David Owl would have one hanging in the springhouse behind his home.

When our parents bought the farm in 1928, the pond didn't exist. My father dug out and dammed up what had been a wide marshy area. He thought to put a little island boat-destination in the middle and, hoping to attract herons, wild ducks, or even egrets, he put in various bird-luring plants like wild rice. It was an aquatic garden that came to naught. He stocked the pond with various fish, but only the catfish and an occasional sunny survived.

The pond provided us with fun year round—swimming, fishing (in spite of the catfish), skating (very special on moonlight nights when we would bring along the wind-up victrola to play Viennese waltzes), tobogganing or sledding down the hill onto the ice, sailing or paddling my little sailboat and exploring up the small stream that fed the pond. At its headland stood the best of all possible climbing trees. We spent hours scaling it and swinging from branch to branch. We liked taking visiting children, especially those we didn't know well, to this tree to show off our prowess and challenge theirs.

At the edge of the woods in a wild meadow area, a favorite picnicking spot with the prettiest view of the pond, stood the remains of a Pennsylvania Dutch house. We called it The Ruin. The walls of its foundation were still intact, filled with the jumble of the building's stones and rife with weeds. We did not venture down into the cellar for fear of snakes.

Picnicking near The Ruin one day when I was some four

years old, sitting with the adults waiting for the chicken to cook over a wood fire, suddenly someone grabbed my hand. We flew—there's no other word for it, my feet barely touched the ground—back on the pathway to The Big House. As I was pulled along I saw the black funnel of a tornado. By the time we took refuge in a cellar, the storm was over. Our stone barn had been blown down. I was not allowed near the site for some time and when I finally could go there workmen were already busy reconstructing the building. I was reminded of this incident some eight years later when The Ruin became the foundation for a new house, one we children might still wish had never been built.

On the southerly side of the road where The Big House sat, and past the various other buildings, the fields for crops and pasture rose up and then sloped down to another woodland, this one quite boggy. It was the best place to catch the early spring. Mayflowers, spring beauties, dogtooth violets, jack-in-the-pulpits abounded there. And skunk cabbage! On a hot summer day this area was cooler than any other place on the farm. A creek meandered through it and at one bend provided a good child-size swimming hole with a pebbly beach. The downside of going for a swim there was the return trek when one got hot and sweaty all over again. I think it was our Indian playmates, the Owls, who gave us the idea of smearing our bodies with mud to keep ourselves cooler. And this meant that when we got home we could be washed off with the garden hose and momentarily feel refreshed once again.

Driving by our place, one would notice the small stone farmhouse—a humble but lovely example of early Pennsylvania Dutch architecture dating back to the late 1600s and said to be a stopping place for George Washington on the night of his famous Delaware crossing. Possibly this was so. For sure, Washington's headquarters then were on the other side of Jericho Mountain. Our friends the Chapins lived there.

The Owl family lived in the stone farmhouse. We rarely went inside it. In the earlier days it contained not a stick of furniture—only a stove in the kitchen and, in the front room, a player piano that belonged to us and provided an excuse for asking, "Can we come in?" The house had no plumbing either for kitchen or bathroom. An outhouse and a pump in the backyard served those purposes. And a springhouse in the meadow beyond was the nearest thing to a refrigerator. It was, in fact, very cool and food could be safely stored there.

Near the farmhouse stood a stone barn built in the same era—an equally simple, beautiful structure sporting a weathervane. After the tornado the vane was gone. Several weeks later it was returned to us by a farmer who found it on his property several miles away. This barn was strung along with the other barn buildings bordering the barnyard. One of the barnyard walls was the base of the so-called playhouse—a place we never played in. Its practical purpose was for spreading out walnuts to dry. Sometimes we slept there. The ground level served as a pigpen. For a while our pig Benjamin was in residence there. He, being the most sociable of pigs, preferred to escape from his porcine quarters and trot up to The Big House, get his back scratched, and root around in the vegetable garden. He once got into the house by prying open the screen door on the front porch and barged in on a teatime gathering in the living room, much to the disapproval of a visiting grandfather. Grandpa Townsend, who never approved of his daughter's farm life, was outraged rather than amused. Benjamin eventually became bacon.

At one of the entrances to the barnyard stood a pair of posts each sporting a wrought-iron owl. They were, unofficially, the farm's mascots. In the late forties an antiques scavenger stole them. I think they ended up perched at the driveway entrance of a house in Farmington, Connecticut, where I spotted their exact likeness some years later.

A passerby perhaps also would notice an odd square gray building halfway between The Big House and the barns. This was the Elephant House, so called because it once housed elephants during the months when a traveling one-ring circus holed up for the winter. Those days were past, but there were some remnants of circus posters on the walls to show any doubting Thomases. In our time, the Elephant House's upper story was a place for drying walnuts. John Deere farm machinery held pride of place where elephants had tramped, and a chicken run lined one side.

We spent a great deal of our time being out-of-doors, familiar with the grounds and buildings of the farm, yet always finding something new to do. We were never at a loss about being occupied. To call us back from wherever we were someone would ring the bell. It hung on a post by the back cellar door by which the Rose Red and Rose White grew. The bell's clang could be heard clearly at the far reaches of our three-hundred-and-fifty-acre property. It was originally meant to alert neighbors to an emergency, principally fire. There now being telephones to serve that purpose, I imagine that our neighbors knew that the sound of the Jacksons' bell meant a summons to the children—time to come home now. And we would.

The Big House, our home, was roomy. The main part was a three-story box made handsome in the front by its porch and the many windows. It adjoined a much smaller two-story section that I suspect was in situ when the "box" was built. This part connected with the clapboard kitchen end. Altogether an architectural hodgepodge.

The double front door, not often used, entered into a large hallway. On one side was our living room; on the other, our father's study, its elaborate long mantelpiece indicating that the room was meant to be the parlor. The study end of the room consisted of a large work table flanked by bookshelves. On it, aside from the big dictionary and the needed writing materials (always among them a pad of yellow legal paper), a little Gandhi carved in wood and wearing a teensy loincloth stood next to a tile of brilliant Indian mosaic. Hanging on a window niche wall was an Audubon print of barn swallows, the kind that nested in our barns and sat on the telephone wire on summer evenings. Our piano was in the study and there we put up the Christmas tree, candlelit, and sang carols with the Owls on Christmas Eve.

At the back of the study a door led out to the Beauty Spot—so Bousie named it after putting it together. There was a patio—paved with Mercer tiles featuring signs of the Zodiac—provided with wrought iron furniture suitable for a tea party. Planted around the patio were beds of glamorous perennials: rhodedendrons, azaleas, arbutus. Unfortunately none of the plantings liked the spot. They grew more scraggly and scrawny from year to year. But the name persisted and once in a blue moon we had tea there.

The stairs going up from the front hall to the floor above

sported a wonderful banister—great for sliding down. On winter mornings, since it was cold up on the third floor where my sisters and I had our bedrooms, we would arm ourselves with our clothes and slide down the banister, the sooner to get dressed and warm up on the grate over the furnace.

A grandfather clock, wound once a week, stood in the front hallway, signaling a lot about the furnishings of our house. Most of them were early American antiques collected by our father for his antique business, which was a failure. In those days there was little appreciation or demand for what he had collected, so much of it ended up in our house. We were definitely short on cozy chairs and plushy sofas. There weren't any.

We were short of, that is we were without, anything resembling central heating. The furnace required a good deal of expert attention to be sure it kept going. But it did not heat the house, it just took some of any winter chill out of the air in its vicinity. We had a Franklin stove in the living room, a coal stove in our father's study and another in the dining room. And then there was the kitchen's large coal range and a number of small portable kerosene space heaters to call into service. We dressed warmly in layers that included the much disliked winter undershirts. Winters back then, once they set in, stayed consistently cold (my father was already talking about global warming).

We were also short in the bathroom department. There was only one. The former owners had taken in summer-vacationing boarders. A little sign about house rules still hung in one of the back rooms. With one bathroom and the fact that the supply of hot water (heated in a tank by the kitchen's coal stove) only sufficed for a bath a few inches deep, one does wonder how everyone managed. They must, at times, have had to trek to the outhouse beyond the vegetable garden. This was supplied with four seats in graduated sizes leading one to imagine an entire family sitting together there to perform the necessary. Just as those boarders managed somehow, we and our visitors did too. And this despite the fact that the paterfamilias commandeered the bathroom every morning and, as we put it, "read on the pot." It was a nice place for reading as it had a wide windowsill with two large windows looking out over the front lawn.

One winter the pipes froze and we had to call the outhouse into service. Our mother cleared out the cobwebs and scrubbed the place up, providing it with candles, a kerosene stove, and a stack of Sears Roebuck catalogs, the big fat ones they used to put out with page on page of brassieres, girdles, tools, shoes to search through in order to locate the things we yearned for— bicycles, music boxes, tents. By the time we had gotten used to the outhouse arrangement, thaw set in and the broken pipes were mended.

Our house was not short on cellars; there were three large ones. One housed the furnace and its coal pile. The walls there were hung with all sorts of antique kitchenware, utensils, and tools and we stored skates, sleds, and the toboggan there too. The deep cellar, a good six feet below the others, was uninviting, clammy, and always cold. Its walls were lined with shelves laden with jars of canned fruits and vegetables, some predating our occupancy of the house by a long shot. This would have been the place to hang a deer, if our father had ever shot one. There he kept a large vat of stew he mixed up weekly for the dogs, and, during the war years, there was a barrel filled with a repugnant jellylike substance that preserved eggs—not an inviting chore to go down to the deep cellar to get a few when needed in the kitchen. At the back end of the house the friendliest cellar served as the laundry; there a chute from the second floor emptied the dirty clothes near the large sinks. It required two people to work the gas-motored washing machine with rubber rollers for wringing out the wash—one to turn the rollers, another to feed in the clothes. This sometimes turned dramatic when someone got a finger or a pigtail caught.

The attic was more enticing than the cellars. We'd sneak up to it on a rainy day. It smelled of dust, cobwebs, wasp bodies, and cedar. There were trunks filled with fancy dresses and Parisian lingerie our mother no longer wore, letters tied up with ribbons, copies of our father's poetry, little white boxes of wedding cake (which we ate), old photographs. In the bureau drawers were tools, pieces of interesting leather, and fine Italian papers for book binding, something our father had tried his hand at. There were vivid paints and gold leaf—don't breathe! (of course we did)—for illuminating manuscripts and stacks of old maps and Pennsylvania Dutch Fraktur, illuminated designs, and pen paintings. We purloined a few attic things and laid claim to them as our own. It was probably reverse justice that someone stole most of my little stash of attic plunder some years later.

It was through our findings in the attic that we began to learn a bit about our forebears. For instance, we came upon a group portrait of the prosperous, elegant Jackson family. We could see our father—the baby—on his pretty mother's lap, his father standing by, his brothers and sisters gathered around, his aunts and uncles there too. Many of the men had balding heads, as did he. And there was an engraving of a handsome officer, one Oliver Wolcott. He had signed the Declaration of Independence, as another ancestor, Samuel Huntington, had as well. As the attic drawers revealed, and as we pieced together answers to questions asked, we had a heritage that explained the deeply felt American patriotism that was rooted in our father's character.

And—I mustn't forget—just off the living room, the Telephone Closet, filled with stuff including Santa Claus supplies near Christmastime, but giving pride of place to the telephone. We were on a party line. When the phone rang four times, the call was for us. We had a very clever parrot, Miranda by name. She knew when the phone was ringing just for us and would call out, "Mrs. Jackson, Mrs. Jackson! Telephone. Telephone, Mrs. Jackson." There was no dial on this phone. One had to wait for the operator's "Number please" to make a phone call and she, as well as the others on the line, could surreptitiously listen in on the conversation. One of our mother's friends found this particularly amusing. She would arrive, throw down her luggage, and dash to the telephone to see what was going on. She was keeping track of an illicit love affair connected with two rings. The erring wife would have conversations with her lover and let him know when the coast was clear.

People liked coming to our place. They always seemed to have a good time being there. There was something unique about its atmosphere. Part of this was due to the everyday elements of our life, which were becoming increasingly of-an-earlier-era. We did not have electricity; our home was illuminated by kerosene lamps and candles. Well-kept kerosene lamps give off a lovely light and no modern lighting compares to a candlelit Christmas tree. We had our own bedside lamps—put your light out *now!* All through the night the lamps on the landings and in the bathroom gave a warm and comforting glow.

Then, there was the icebox—boxes in summer when an extra was put to use. This meant the regular appearance of the iceman and the don't-forget-to-empty-the-drip-pans under the icebox. The iceman came infrequently in the winter but several times a week in summertime. Along with the iceman, until the early forties, there were also the breadman who had a side-line of pies and wonderful sticky cinnamon buns; the butcher; the fishmonger, who came regularly on Fridays; and the knife-sharpener, who turned up before any major holiday when a turkey or roast beef were slated for the oven.

It took ingenuity to cook on our large coal-burning kitchen range. When fast action was called for, wood was added, to get things going in the morning or to heat up the irons for iron-ing, tricky to get just right so that the iron in use was not too hot, and, when it became too cool, the next iron was ready. The Owl children liked to drop corn worms on the stove top and let them become brown and crisp for a pop-in-the-mouth treat. Probably delicious but we were too squeamish to try them.

When the cows gave us a surfeit of heavy cream, we would call an old butter churn into service. When the big treat of ice cream was planned, out came the old ice-cream maker, the ice pick, the rock salt, and a big chunk of ice from the icebox. Our radio was powered by a car-size battery; our record player, for which we had all of Beethoven's symphonies and a stash of country-western and cowboy songs (I especially remember "See the True and Trembling Brakeman") ordered from Sears Roebuck, had to be wound up every few minutes before allegro turned to largo. It had shutters on the sides for adjusting the volume.

In other words we were not quite up to date. Somehow there was something more adventurous about the implements of our daily lives then than seems the case with the light switch, the pop-up toaster, the microwave, the giant supermarkets, the tires that don't need chains to get through snowy roads, the cell phones that make instant connections—the long list of gadgets that today make our lives easier and more alacritous but a good deal less endearing. The truth is that candles and lamps give out a nicer light, that laboriously churned ice cream has a more delicious taste, that little country dirt roads were prettier and more adventurous to drive on. I feel fortunate to have known such long-ago things, appreciated then by all of us and by visiting family and friends, many of whom have fond memories of times on our farm. Our not-up-to-dateness was one of its charms.

PEOPLE

It is difficult to sift through my childhood perceptions of my parents from all I pieced together or speculated on in later years. A child does not pause to analyze or map out the separate life stories of his or her mother and father. It is only as time goes by that one finds, if one explores the matter, what they did or had done aside from being parents. As a child, as far as I was concerned, I neither saw nor heard anything that implied they weren't a pair that fit together and I never felt that everything wasn't as fine in their lives as it was in mine. If they had disagreements or worries, such were never apparent to me.

We called our father "Bousie" (rhymes with Howsie). How that name came about I don't know. A time arrived when he didn't want us to address him as Bousie anymore. None of us could change it in our minds or when speaking of him. "Dear Father" just did not, and still doesn't, equate with "Dear Bousie." And he was a very dear father. He never changed a diaper or held a baby bottle as fathers often do nowadays, but he was very involved with us. He was the king as far as we were concerned and we adored him. He did not indulge or spoil us in the least, in fact he tended to be somewhat judgmental. But he treasured us and he made our lives not only interesting but often exciting.

There were his little touches—a bright ribbon or a pressed

flower turning up in the book one was reading at the time; a golden feather dropped on the dollhouse floor, the food left for the fairies gone.

A more elaborate example of Bousie's touch. I had set myself up to sell apples. Never mind that the apples, ill-shaped and wormy, came from the seedy orchard near our vegetable garden. No matter that very few potential customers would be driving by. There I sat at the lawn's edge in high hopes. A long time passed. Only one car came by and it did not stop. This was getting boring. Then—hobbling, leaning on a cane, came a little old woman well wrapped up in musty shawls. I had a customer! With a crackling voice, the crone asked for three apples and presented me with a shiny piece of silver. Only after she hobbled off did it dawn on me that she was Bousie.

For a time Bousie went up to New York during the week, coming home on the weekends. He'd always bring us something. One time it was halvah in round tin cans; another, it was honeydew melons—we'd never seen them before. He had carved each one with our individual names. All his presents had a special touch; but Peanuts was the big surprise. Home again and Bousie seemed to be empty-handed. We waited, but nothing. All hopeful expectations evaporated. He suggested we take a little walk. And then! Then, lo and behold, from inside his jacket he produced a tiny dog—a runty poodleish creature he had bought from someone selling a litter of mutt puppies on a New York City street.

Peanuts was an enchanting little being. We fell in love with him. He was the pet of pets. I don't know how long we had him before the terrible accident. We were all sitting on the front porch for teatime and along the road came a car, a fairly rare occurrence unless it was our own. We heard the screech of brakes, the car stopped, and then across the lawn a man came carrying the limp body of our pet. Bousie knew how to channel our sorrow. He organized a stately funeral ceremony by the cedar tree next to the front porch. He played his pan pipe—there always must be music on such occasions. Peanuts, wrapped in a fine piece of cloth, was buried in grand and solemn style, his little grave bedecked with flowers we put there over the following weeks.

Our mother dealt with the more practical side of things: buttoning up overcoats, making us wear undershirts, taking care of us when we were sick—we all remember being plied with castor oil and other medicines, bad-tasting as medicine always was back then, teaching us to shake hands and curtsy when greeting grownups, running the household. Early on we called her "Muddy," a variation I suppose of the German "Mutti" (probably inherited from Fraulein, the German governess who took care of my mother and her siblings, when they were growing up). At some point Muddy became Ma. We counted on her to "be there" and she was.

What I remember most clearly about my childhood feeling regarding her are the times when I became worried that she wouldn't "be there." The first of these was on a boat in Newport. I'm three years old. The boat is racing along. Stretching behind it is a rope at the end of which my mother rides on a water board. I'm terrified that she's going to get lost. Or is she going to drown? Another time she's been stung by a wasp or a bee (she has honeybees in hives near our vegetable garden). One eye is completely swollen shut, her whole face is discolored and bloated. Will it get worse? Or an accident; she has spilled a pan of boiling water—well, actually a pan of something to do with beer-making—and scalded her legs. Will she be all right? There would come a time when I had every reason to believe she would not.

I called my sisters and brother "the kids" and thought of them really as *my* kids. I clearly remember the day each was born.* Maria's birth I have mentioned already. By the time I was ten, Maria was catching up with me in the sense that the gap between our ages seemed narrower. We began sharing many things together and would do so particularly when the terrible summer came along.

The six-year age difference between me and my sister Kathie meant she was not a confidante as Maria became. I visualize now the night Kathie was born. She was late in coming. A trained nurse in full white uniform had been on hand for several weeks. In the hallway outside the bathroom a bathinette stood ready. An air of something-about-to-happen hovered. That night I knew, though not exactly why, that kettles were on the stove to boil water. Dr. Leiby, who delivered all my siblings, was coming. My mother took me upstairs to the third floor to tuck me in bed. Halfway up I became aware, for the first time, of her protruding belly. I felt she was being brave in her condition, as well as especially kind, to be lumbering up the stairs with me. When I woke the next morning, there was the new baby.

Kathie was the shyest one of us and she refused to speak a word until she was some two years old. Then all of a sudden,

---

* I was born in a fancy lying-in hospital in New York City but our mother so disliked the experience of giving birth under the twilight sleep approach practiced there then that she had the rest of her babies at home, Dr. Leiby in attendance and a trained nurse on hand to help with the baby for the first weeks.

having been asked something, she sonorously uttered one. Instead of the usual nod one way or the other she said, "No!" "She can talk, she can talk!" we exclaimed. And indeed she could for, after that one little word, Kathie made it clear that she had a hefty working vocabulary and had just been biding her time until she was good and ready to use it.

My brother was born on a rainy June night. My father and I sat on the window seat in one of the little rooms in the middle section of the house and, while we sat, the rain stopped, the sky cleared, and the stars came out. We picked one star and wished on it for a boy baby. Sure enough, soon after that the wish came true.

He was given his father's name, Schuyler, an awkward one for a little tyke. We called him Skylie but that didn't sit well. It didn't suit a little fellow so full of energy, racing around and making a hubbub, diapers always threatening to fall off. The moniker seemed sissy. An aunt came to visit and, on her return to England where she lived, she sent each of us a postcard. The one for Schuyler had this message: "Here's a picture of the Big Ben in London for the Little Ben in Brownsburg." Immediately everyone agreed—"Let's call him Ben."

I often tried to marshall my forces, the kids—their preparedness being at varying levels and sometimes hampering my success as a general. One day I decided we should run away from home. The idea was inspired by the notion of having an adventure more than by dissatisfaction with the homefront. Each of us had something that would do as a bindle stick and off we set. Ben, still in diapers and having not the foggiest notion of what he was supposed to be doing, was left behind a few steps from the back porch. By the time we got to the laundry line, fluttering with sheets hung out to dry, Kathie became tearfully homesick and was sent back in disgrace. Maria and I trudged through the fields and up the hill. At the crest, Maria looked back, decided that home was the better option, and left me to run away by myself. I plodded on over to the Peacocks' farm, where I found a tree to sit in before undertaking the next leg of the journey. The sun began to set and the idea of life on the road along with it. And what would the kids do without me, I wondered, searching for a rationale for abandoning the adventure. I got down from my perch and slogged home, arriving just in time for supper. The troops, traitors all, had been happily busy without me, their general. I felt quite left out and unappreciated and suffered a case of hurt feelings, only cheering up when dessert turned out to be prune whip with custard sauce.

In general we were well-behaved children. The main trouble was the fighting that erupted now and then. I was usually above the fray but Maria and Kathie had at it sometimes and Ben and Kathie rather often. Indeed, the latter were so prone to flareups for a while that our parrot Miranda learned to imitate them in battle and our mother sometimes would rush into the living room—"Now you two cut it out"—and find no one there but the bird. And once when she was entertaining a few ladies for tea, the cook came in to say matter-of-factly, "Mrs. Jackson, Ben is chasing Kathie with an ax." The ladies, one of whom was a teacher checking up on the home scene, were startled, as well they might be. This intersibling warfare was only a passing stage, similar to the establishment of a pecking order in a hen yard.

As far as we children were concerned, our family included

the people who helped on the farm and in our house. They made up, most especially the Cherokee Indians, the rest of our home family.

David Owl came, as it were, with the place. Cherokee Indians from the reservation in North Carolina's Smoky Mountains—the band that eluded the Trail of Tears forced march to Oklahoma—came north every year to New Jersey and Pennsylvania looking for work at harvest time. David and his brothers Tom, Sam, and Quincey had been regularly coming to the farm before it became ours. When our father met David he asked him if he would like to bring his family up, move into the stone farmhouse, and have a permanent job helping with the farm work. This was an opportunity above and beyond the usual prospect a Cherokee on the reservation could look forward to. Most of them, as my mother once remarked, were too poor to buy so much as a 3-cent stamp.

David was a handsome, dignified, mild-mannered, hardworking man. He took things calmly and often with humor. Our father, a hard worker himself, could not have managed without him.

For me, David was like a second father. Often, early mornings or late afternoons, I would trot around after him while he did the barnyard chores, the last of which usually was milking the cows, eventually the one cow—our pet, Sally by name. I'd perch on a hay bale or an upturned bucket and David and I would converse to the plinking and plunking of milk into the pail, with the barn cats in a row expectantly waiting for a squirt while we chewed the rag. We had many serious discussions. We talked about all sorts of things. I was full of questions that I felt David could and would answer for me. I asked him about God—where was He, what was He like? David told me God was a good presence enveloping the world, the universe. He told me that when a person really needed Him, God would be there. His belief in this was deeply felt and it made good sense to me.

Next to my father, whom David loved dearly all his life, he thought the world of Franklin Delano Roosevelt. What, I wonder now, had F.D.R. ever done for the band of North Carolina Cherokee Indians or, for that matter, any of the American Indians? Nonetheless he commanded David's fealty. Perhaps Roosevelt gave out a great sense of hope for the future, a belief that things would one day be better. Some years after leaving the farm, David and Mae had another child. He was named Franklin Delano Roosevelt Owl (with an e added so that Owl became Owle from then on).

I asked David many questions about the Cherokee and I tried to learn some of the language. The only word I still remember is "shellagadoo," cornbread. The serious side of our discussions about the Cherokee led to a ceremony, one I don't think I told anyone about at the time. It was a very private matter between just the two of us, not in any sense a game. David conducted a blood-brother ceremony with me. It took place in the barnyard by the water trough in the corner where the wrought-iron owls graced the doorposts. David sterilized a needle over a kitchen match, pricked both of our fingers, and held them together while he said some words in Cherokee. Something happened. To this day I can sense the presence of an Indian person. Believe it or not, there is some call of the blood at work.

This ceremony took place in the fall. The next spring, after

David came back from the yearly Cherokee powwow (I believe, in fact, that he was the tribal chief at that time, a position later held by his brother Tom), he brought me a gift, a talisman confirming my induction into the Cherokee Nation. He told me that he had put me before the Council and that I was now an elected Cherokee princess, and he gave me a headdress with a beaded band, four eagle feathers, and pompoms decorated with little ermine tails at the sides. I hardly need say that this remains one of my treasures.

David was a steady, meticulous worker on the farm, sharing a heavy work load with Bousie. Days off were rare, but once in a while we'd have a treat David shared in. A trip to distant Flemington (all of maybe fifteen miles away) to see *Gone With the Wind*, up to New York for a glimpse of the World's Fair; most of the way to Philadelphia to see a baseball game canceled by rain; or something as simple as a ride on the back of the farm truck—one ride in particular. There we children all were, some seven or eight of us, perched on top of a stack of hay bales. David went over a sudden bump and we, children and hay bales, flew together into the air and down to the ground in a heap. No one injured. David laughed his head off at the sight of us, making us forget that we had received some large "ows."

David's wife, Mae, may have had some Indian blood but, if so, it didn't show in her looks. She was redheaded and had very pale skin. She was the first person I saw nursing her baby (that would have been Lillian, later renamed Sylvia). Whenever I think of her I can see her sitting on a large boulder by the big barn door, Lillian at her breast.

David and Mae had three girls—Darleena and Polly (the most

Indian looking) our constant playmates, and Lillian/Sylvia the baby. It was a second marriage for both. Sometimes we saw Lloyd, a very handsome fellow, and Caldonia from David's first wife and Mae's son John, called J.H. (later J.O.), was a permanent member of the family.

Two other permanent members of the family were Mae's two younger brothers, Jean and A.B. Shook. Jean was about J.H.'s age and my sister Maria's fishing companion. She and Jean would stock a tin can with worms and set off for the pond or the swimming hole. Sometimes they actually caught a fish. What might have been a budding romance was later nipped in the bud, our mother worried they might be getting too close. A.B. was well into puberty and really a bit too old to be playing with the rest of us. He had s-e-x on his mind and was frustrated that we weren't particularly interested. He had a treasured comic book showing the Katzenjammer kids up to hanky-panky in the hayloft, but it seemed that David or Mae always knew when he was putting it on display and took it away. Sometimes in the summer A.B. would be stationed down by the pond dam with the ice-cream maker, a bag of rock salt, a block of ice, and an ice pick. And there he would sit dreamily churning away at a snail's pace. If A.B. was making ice cream, a full morning would be allotted for the task.

We Jackson children thought it was very funny that so-near-of-an-age Jean and A.B. were in fact the Owl children's uncles. Their father Mr. Shook stayed on the farm for a year or so. His main activity, weather permitting, was to sit in a rocking chair in the middle of the stone-house lawn reading either the Bible or the Want Ads in the romance section of some pulp magazine. He was, we knew, waiting for replies to an ad he had placed. He had applied for a wife and indeed one of the respondents filled the bill. Mr. Shook took off to get married, leaving his sons behind. Perhaps the bride wanted no encumbrances.

As for the other people who helped us, Mrs. Billings and Pauline Allen, both from nearby Brownsburg, were longtime regulars. Mrs. Billings had a large family of her own— ten or more children, including a son doing time in the workhouse, as jail for juvenile delinquents was called, and a banty-cock husband with tell tale signs of too much drink and no particular job to pay for it. Mrs. Billings showed no signs of stress over her home situation and somehow found time to wash and iron our great heaps of laundry and especially to help out on short notice when we came down with various childhood diseases in those prevaccination, pre-antibiotics times. She had the makings of a fine trained nurse—just her presence made everything better. She'd tidy things up, fluff the pillows, give us our medicine, take temperatures, give pigeon baths and witchhazel rubdowns, bring up trays laden with food and drink. It was the very lap of luxury having Mrs. Billings take care of one in the clutch of measles, mumps, chickenpox, grippe.

Pauline Allen helped in the kitchen and with the general housework. She was a friendly presence. I used to discuss my romantic interests with her and she would throw some down-to-earth on my declarations about J.O. We had a million-dollar bet, the most money we could imagine then, on whether I would marry him. I owe her the money yet. I think Pauline was on hand the night when everything fell apart. What could she have thought of it?

Cooks came and went in our house rather frequently. We had

good, simple food of the meat, potato, and vegetable kind and if-you-don't-clean-your-plate-no-dessert desserts. They were called floating island, prune whip, George Washington's cake, snow pudding, Indian pudding, apple Betty. We cleaned our plates. Occasionally cleaning plates was a struggle, the worst being with okra, which Bousie planted one summer. It was boiled solo, not the best way to handle that vegetable. Maria particularly had a hard time getting down even one forkful and urpsed it up, thereby getting us all an okra reprieve. The best dessert ever, to my mind, was the rice pudding a Swedish cook made for us. It was so delicious that I would sneak down the back stairs leading to the pantry and filch extra helpings. I have since been presented with other rice puddings and myself tried every recipe that has come my way and none have come close to hers. Perhaps it was partly due to the long, slow cooking on our coal stove.

Some of our cooks didn't know how to cook. Our mother, who didn't know how to cook then either, taught them by giving them The Fannie Farmer Cookbook. At least one of the cooks did not know how to read. That was a Cherokee by the wonderful name of Waygee Katolster. How she produced a meal is anyone's guess. We were intrigued by her, as she was full of Indian lore and also rather crazy. She was fearful of looking ceiling-ward because, if she did, she would see her mother, of whom she was terrified, and she had a thing about snakes that were threatening her and us as well, whether we believed it or not. She went into trances, observed by us peeking down through the grate in the kitchen ceiling. I don't think our meals worked out too well when Waygee was the chef.

Earlier we had another Cherokee woman working in our

kitchen. This was Mrs. Squirrel, who came with her daughter Dinah, an early playmate of mine. Dinah came back to us for a short stretch some years later. After she left, she wrote our mother to tell her that she had stolen some jewelry and, now that she had become a born-again Christian, was confessing and apologizing. Sad to say, Dinah Squirrel was fated to die along with Lloyd Owl in a car crash some years later.

Then there was Elizabeth, an Irish woman, also with a daughter. Elizabeth introduced us to Irish stew and me to the Catholic Church. Not having been taken to church before, as far as I knew, I was impressed. One particular homily sticks in my mind. It was about the evil of women wearing pants. The priest got very riled up on the subject. I liked wearing blue jeans and always changed into them when I got home from school. What wearing or not wearing pants had to do with such things as the holy-water fount, which Elizabeth would not allow me to dip my finger in and then make the sign of the cross, was beyond my grasp. Still is.

Elizabeth was very concerned about my baby sister Kathie, who had not been baptised. She took the opportunity to remedy this situation during a violent thunderstorm. She grabbed Kathie from the crib and ran out into the downpour, lightning, and thunder, and, oblivious to the danger, conducted her own christening ceremony. So far as I know Maria and I were still unbaptized heathens, but I suppose from Elizabeth's point of view it was too late to do anything about that. At least one baby had been saved from perdition.

And there was the Georgia peach of a girl—Marie. As I remember her, she was right up there with Marilyn Monroe. We spied on her through the grate in the kitchen ceiling. We knew that David's son Lloyd fancied her and we hoped to see some romantic doings when he brought in the coal for the kitchen stove or the milk up from the barn. Lloyd did not get far along with his suit since his courtship was interrupted by a horrible accident. When he was working with the buzz saw splitting wood for the winter woodpile—maybe even then dreaming of the Georgia Peach—he severed a hand. Soon after this tragedy he left the farm and later shared the fate of Dinah Squirrel.

On Sunday nights (Sunday midday dinner being the big meal of the week, usually with a roast) Bousie was often the cook. His specialty was scrambled eggs and these were The Best. He used just a little bit of cream and huge amounts of butter and he cooked the eggs on the coolest part of the stove, stirring constantly for a very long time. Like the aforementioned rice pudding, Bousie's scrambled eggs have not been duplicated.

Our kitchen was about as far a cry away from a modern one as one could get. No stainless steel, chrome, formica, marble. Instead, the large wood/coal-burning range, one shallow sink with a narrow wooden drain board, two banks of cupboards with sticky doors and drawers, and an array of tables covered with oilcloth. All of us have fond memories of times there. One cook made doughnuts and fried up the holes for us to eat. We had some riotous taffy pulls and some disastrous fudge making. And there were many chances to lick the bowls in which cake and cookies had been mixed. Gustatory matters aside, the grate in the ceiling provided a peephole we found adventurous to use, even when there was nothing particular to spy on in the kitchen below.

Annetta was not a cook, although she sometimes pitched in. Her main job was taking care of the kids. I was a little too old to be her charge so for me she was more like a friend and, since I too took care of the kids, so I felt, a colleague. She came to us from a farm in western Pennsylvania, one Maria and I visited one Easter vacation and found just like a farm in a picture book. Annetta reminded us of Mary Poppins—in the book, not the movie. It was easy to imagine that, if she chose to, she could perfectly well slide up the banister, both flights up to the third floor where her room was along with mine and my sisters' plus the linen closet. It wasn't just her looks, but her manner that brought Miss Poppins to mind. She exceeded Mary P. in the beaux department though—no lone Bert for her. How she met them is a mystery, but she had a number of suitors. There was the next thing to a duel on our front lawn late one night. Annetta was being brought home from a date by one of her boyfriends. Another was lying in wait behind the rambling rose bush by the driveway. Bousie, in his pajamas, had to break up the serious fight that ensued.

Annetta, prim and proper though her mien, "got into trouble," as it was put back then. She went off to Trenton one morning—I think David drove her, heaven knows to what sort of place. She was home by midafternoon and set to work weeding in the garden, tears rolling down her face, her shoulders heaving from suppressed sobs. I was very upset about her and cross at my mother who I thought was being cruel to make Annetta work. I can't fathom how I knew what had gone on. Did I piece things together later, the picture of our sad Annetta etched in my mind?

Annetta left us to take up a teaching position. Later she happily married a prosperous farmer who had not been one of her earlier suitors. She never had any children, a pity. Perhaps because of the trip to Trenton.

SCHOOL DAYS

I have a slight recollection of being in what must have been a nursery school. Bright new blocks and pull toys; little chairs in gaudy primary colors. But the first schooling I clearly remember was in a one-room schoolhouse some two miles away from the farm and situated on a hilltop. I must have been driven there some of the time but my memory is of the walk to and from—first on the dirt road, then the macadam. I was five and my father was no doubt thinking that if Abraham Lincoln could walk to school, so could I. On the last stretch of the dirt road before it joined the macadam, a bridge crossed the stream meandering through the Slacks' meadow—the Slack family being on the farm neighboring ours, a farm provided with a bull that our cows visited when the time came. On my trek to school the bridge was a challenge far outweighing that of the steep uphill climb on the last third of the journey to the schoolhouse. It was equally challenging on the way home. I had the idea that an unfriendly troll might be lurking under it or that I would encounter the bull on it. And one day there *was* a bovine creature standing on the bridge. It was undoubtedly not the bull, who was nasty-tempered and kept corralled up, but I was too frightened to cross over and hid by the roadside—I couldn't sneak under the bridge because the troll was there—until my mother came along and rescued me. By that time the animal had strayed away.

The daily apprehension about getting over the bridge past trolls and bulls was worth enduring, because I thought school was wonderful. The pretty, plump, and cheerful Miss Rossiter managed to keep everyone busy. It seems to me I was mostly busy with a coloring book. Somehow coloring in school was tinged with an excitement not felt at home.

How long I would have continued to feel delighted who knows, but my school days there were of short duration. One fine day as I was trotting along the way to school, swinging my lunch box and the little book bag holding my coloring book and pencils, a car pulled up beside me and a small bespectacled man asked me if I would like a lift as he too was going to the school I must be heading for. Without a moment's hesitation I popped up onto the seat beside him and off we drove. Nowadays one would immediately assume the man was up to no good, but that was not the case, nor likely to be so. No warnings had been issued about accepting such favors from strangers. People thumbing rides got them. And if they didn't thumb a driver would, more often than not, stop and offer a lift. It turned out that this man was the county school inspector and in our conversation en route to the school he discovered that I was five years old and would not be turning six until after the new year. He was a prissy sort of fellow and he tut-tutted at this disclosure. It was against regulations for a five-year-old to attend public school and my protestations that I knew my alphabet and the numbers only evoked a tongue-clicking sound from him and a readjustment of his spectacles, which had slipped down his nose a bit. We arrived at the schoolhouse.

The inspector had some words with Miss Rossiter, there were tears, and I was sent homeward immediately, in disgrace for my unacceptable lack of the proper age.[*]

I am not sure that I went to school at all for first and second grade. For third through fifth grades though I went to a school in New Hope, one depicted in a late nineteenth-century painting, *Manchester Valley*, by the folk artist Joseph Pickett.

Bousie would drop me off at the foot of the hill and I would join the little parade trudging up it. One snowy winter day it was not clear whether school was open or not. Bousie enjoined me to climb up and, once at the top, to send him a signal. If school was not in session, then I was to put my fingers in each ear and wiggle them. If school was open, then I was to put my thumb on my nose and wiggle my fingers. All the way up the hill I agonized over the possible choice that lay ahead, one more embarrassing than the other. What would my schoolmates think? But Bousie's wish was my command. School was in session.

This stretch of school-going was filled with adventures and is remembered with fondness by most or possibly all of the children who shared them. We sat at little wooden desks with built-in inkwells that actually, at least some of the time, had ink in them. Once a day we lined up and marched into the next-door classroom while its occupants traded rooms with us. I acquired the nickname "Jellybean" because my weekly allowance was generally spent at the candy counter of the little store near the foot of the hill on which the school perched and across from the small creek there. Five cents bought a generous

---

[*] I set foot in that school house once again: in 1948 I cast my first vote there in the presidential election. No voting machine. Instead a wooden box into which one slipped the piece of paper naming one's choice.

cache of candies and my friends looked forward to my allowance day. For many of them such days did not exist. They came from families of slender or even less means and no pennies to spare. In those days the New Hope paper mill was the principle source of available work and one can be sure that hourly wages were small indeed.

Instead of Jellybean I might more appropriately have been dubbed Miss Storyteller for I was an inveterate exaggerater of facts and I often embroidered things with a good deal of baloney. The fact that almost all of my classmates lived in the town and I lived on a farm down the river intrigued them. In my descriptions how mansionlike, even castlelike my house became, how lakelike the pond, how Texas-big the flock of sheep. And all this was nothing to what I'd seen on my travels to foreign places and my knowledge of a number of foreign languages—naturally I had learned them. The curious thing was that when my classmates came to the farm, as they did for a number of parties, they didn't seem to find any discrepancy worth noting between my descriptions and the reality. (Four years later, when I rejoined them in high school for two years, I dreaded being confronted with my stories—now I saw them as lies. The moment of truth came in a history or geography class when the teacher asked if anyone had been to Europe or had studied any foreign languages. "Griselda has," several of them said and I had to confess that I had not been a traveler to foreign lands. That was the end of it. No one seemed to mind in the least.)

In third grade, my first year at this school, I had a crush on Chubby Oblinger. The feeling was mutual. Though we hardly spoke a word to each other, we knew we liked each other. But come fourth grade all this changed with the arrival of Leta Oblinger, Chubby's cousin from the big city—Philadelphia. I had definitely lost out. I still had the crush on him and his way, naturally, to put an end to that was every now and then to be mean, as we called it when someone wasn't being nice. His desk was behind mine. I don't think he dipped my pigtails in the inkwell but he certainly gave them a sharp tug now and then. He was in the marching-to-the-other-classroom line right behind me and his sharp knee in my butt was the norm until one day I lost my temper and turned on him, arms and legs flailing. The teacher could not understand what was afoot. I got sent to the storeroom where the books and supplies were kept along with unruly children.

The storeroom served another purpose one day other than housing supplies and the occasional naughty pupil. We had all been invited to bring a pet to school. I brought Tessie, a lamb we were raising on a bottle, but there was no place to confine her. In the outhouse? That wouldn't do. That left the storeroom, where she was shut in and wreaked some havoc until the afternoon pet contest, in which she won the blue ribbon in the most unusual pet category.

I didn't give up on trying to regain Chubby's affection, my most drastic ploy being the acquisition of eyeglasses. Cousin Leta wore them. If I did, perhaps that would even the field. I nagged my mother, telling her I couldn't see very clearly and was getting headaches. "Read the letters on the chart," the oculist said. "A M Z T D O R" says I, misreading each of the clearly visible letters. Consultation between oculist and mother. I am indulged. I get a pair of glasses appropriate for a person with 20/20 vision. Love remains unrequited, in fact Chubby has had it and knocks me down while the class is on a nature walk (I still have a scar on my knee from the tumble). It sobered me up, though, and when Chubby got seriously ill—typhoid fever I think if was—I left a present, a picture puzzle, at his door, plastered with an "in quarantine" sign, with a note saying I hoped he'd get better and that he would at least like me a little now.

Fifty years later I received a letter—what a surprise!— from Chubby, he having found out my married name and address from another classmate on one of his trips back to New Hope. He wrote that he felt badly for not being so nice to me all those years ago. I had indeed picked well in the object of my affections. On several occasions in recent years when I have seen Chubby (now called Fred; he was never in fact chubby) and some of those long-ago classmates they make me feel good—proud of how we were and how our different lives have developed. We all felt that the school experience, especially the teachers, had been of central importance in our lives; opening up the world, grounding us in it, encouraging our aspirations, nurturing a sense of community and of freedom. I think way back then, when we sang "land of the free" we felt it in our very bones.

My best friend in this school was Margaret Fitzgerald— Fitzie. I had a sleep-over at her home, a trailerlike house on a hill just below New Hope. Fitzie's father worked the night shift at the paper mill. I don't remember how many of us there were together in one big bed for the night, but I think at least five or six. It was a great adventure for me. Fitzie already had a hope chest as did many of the girls in my class. In them were put linens and other things for a future household. By the time of the high school years, many of the girls had settled on the boys they would eventually marry, Fitzie among them. As far as I know, all of these marriages lasted.

After fifth grade I was transferred from the New Hope school. The days of the one-room schoolhouse in Bucks County were numbered and my father thought being in one was an experience that should be grabbed while there was still the opportunity to do so. So for sixth grade I went, along with some twenty-two other children, to Mrs. Leedom's domain on the other side of Jericho Mountain. I marvel now at how Mrs. Leedom managed. Her salary was probably about thirty-five dollars a month and for this paltry sum she was to teach children in eight grades and prepare them for high school. In those days one did not graduate on to a higher grade unless one had passed the basic requirements. So there was Walter, seventeen and still stuck in eighth grade. And there was my lone classmate, Charlie, who was certainly several years older than me. His problem was arithmetic and he assiduously cribbed from my work papers. He happened to be one of the two black students in the school. Let me assure the reader that this made no more difference to anyone than a pile of beans. In our Christmas pageant he was the Santa Claus and I was completely mystified that this bothered my friend Mr. Yeomans of Southern Pines, North Carolina who happened to call on the school while the pageant was in progress. When I told him that the boy was my classmate, I could see that this upset him some. He just wasn't used to such an idea. He became so later.

Mrs. Leedom was short, buxom, and bosomy, wore a stern-looking rimless pince-nez, and never missed a day of school. For the school day she provided everything one can think of as well as teaching each grade in varying sessions. When she was teaching classes other than one's own, one did the work assigned or homework or read books from the little library—that was a bookshelf provided with Nancy Drew mysteries, the Bobsey twins stories, and stray aging classics like *The Last of the Mohicans*. We saluted the flag and sang "My Country, 'Tis of thee," we had a singalong ("Come, Come, Come to the Church in the Wild Wood," "Darling, You Are Growing Old," "The Old Oaken Bucket," "The Daring Young Man on the Flying Trapeze.") We had recesses and lunchtime before which we lined up at the pump (the pumper assigned weekly) and washed our hands with Lifebuoy soap. We had storytime after lunch when all was quiet while Mrs. Leedom read the next chapter. We had *The Weekly Reader*—perhaps the school board provided that. We made Thanksgiving turkeys, Valentines, Mother's Day baskets (all from materials Mrs. Leedom would supply from her own pocket). We had the Christmas pageant and a May pole. We even had some sports, mostly baseball. During one game Walter's pitch hit Mrs. Leedom on the forehead—it seemed that maybe he intended it to, and this was the only time Mrs. Leedom lost her cool. She could not apply any of her standard disciplinary measures to Walter. Tap him on the hand with a ruler? Send him to stand in the corner, dunce's hat on his head? Have him write some exculpatory phrase over one hundred times—and neatly! We went in for storytime and she began to weep. If a pin had been dropped, we would have heard it. We all sat in utter silence and pained concern. Walter, the school's tough guy, stood up and apologized. It was a moment of true drama.

We learned a lot in Mrs. Leedom's school. When I went on to the Quaker school in Lahaska for seventh and eighth grades there were many things I had picked up from overhearing Mrs.

Leedom's tutelage of the higher grades—aspects of American history and world geography, *Evangeline*, scenes from *Hamlet* had as it were osmosed.

Behind the school building, which was literally one room, there was a one-seater outhouse. To "go" one raised one's hand and announced one's need. Some would loiter on this errand, among them Kathie, who was quite miserable being in first grade, and who would no sooner return from the outhouse trip than she would raise her hand again. I think she did not last out more than a week or so. Maria must have been there too but, feeling the weight of my sixth-grade status over her lowly third, I paid no attention to her during the school day and can't visualize her being there.

There are a few students I still remember aside from Walter. One was Wilfred, a thin and scrawny little boy who was very sad. He came from a struggling farm family and was much picked on in school. When he was given a birthday present of a warm winter jacket in May, he wore it proudly to school for all to see and even Mrs. Leedom remarked teasingly about it. Poor Wilfred, I think he was doomed to have bad luck and a miserable life. When the county health inspector paid the twice-yearly visit, Wilfred was among those who had lice. Lice! Scissors came out, hair was shorn, purple medicine was applied with a silent message of disgrace.

Then there was a plump mama's boy, something Cadwalader, who thought he was a good cut above the rest of us—his mother had undoubtedly told him so. He came to school but was not supposed to get chummy with the motley crew. Rather a tricky task, but he did it.

And there was the other black student, Margaret Toomer,

who lived barely half a mile from the school on our route home and lived in fear of us riding by with our father at the wheel. Bousie would always offer her a lift. This struck terror in her—she could barely whisper no. My father was sometimes a naughty tease and this was the case with Margaret. He thought he was being funny, but she was scared of him. Margaret's father was Jean Toomer, the writer, I do believe not a happy or sociable person. Certainly Margaret was neither at that point in her life.

For seventh and eighth grades I went with Maria, Kathie, and Ben to the Buckingham Friends' School in Lahaska. It was a fine small institution lodged in a handsome old stone building with a nearby Quaker meetinghouse which we trouped to several times a month. There was a somewhat sanctimonious quality about that, so it seemed to me. We would sit in silence waiting for the spirit to move someone to say a few words. But the same speakers always seemed to be the ones to pop up and their words often seemed premeditated, truth to tell.

It was a good ten miles or more from our house to school. Bousie usually drove us there. When we got to the last stretch past New Hope, he often drove at breakneck speed, passing the few other cars irrespective of oncoming traffic while we sat on the edge of our seats. There was some reward for the speed—hitting the ups and downs of the road, just right, provided a roller-coaster moment. Once in a while he would take a quick turn off the road and we'd stop to look at the watercress in an artesian spring. Then back on our way again and more bat-out-of-hell driving. Our mother usually was the one who fetched us at the end of the school day.

My little brother Ben did not last long at Buckingham

Friends'. He was not progressing with learning to read and write and one day he discovered that a broken pocket watch he'd acquired could catch the sunlight and reflect it on the teacher's face. Reprimands had no effect. The principal, Miss Randolph, phoned my parents and told them to come immediately and take Ben home. He was suspended. Since the punishment didn't really seem to fit the crime, Ben never returned to that school after the fateful morning. Mrs. Leedom, it must be said, would have taken care of the matter. She had no phone for summoning a parent. She would have marched Ben up to the dunce's corner to sit, dunce cap on head, for a goodly stretch. She had meted that punishment out to me on one occasion and it served its purpose—what an endless afternoon!

There were excellent teachers and classes at Buckingham Friends' School. Here's an interesting science project as it was reported on my all-capitals typewriter under the heading:

NEWS, NEWS, NEWS OF EVERY ONE, EVERWHERE...

AT SCHOOL THE SEVETH GRADE LAST AUTUMN BURIED A DEAD SKUNCK HOPING TO UNCOVER ITS BONES IN THE SPRING. BUT WHEN THEY UNCOVERED IT, MUCH TO THEIR SURPRISE THEY FOUND NO BONES. SO THEY COVERED IT OVER AGAIN AND REPLACED THE GRAVE STONE THEY HAD SO CARE FULLY PAINTED BROWN WITH PINK LETTERS, SAYING HERE LIES MATILDA. BURIED BY THE SEVENT GRADE.

Beyond the good teachers and interesting curriculum, Buckingham Friends was where I developed some short-lived thespian aspirations. First off, I was chosen to be the Madonna in the Christmas pageant and carry the baby Jesus down the meetinghouse aisle, giving him a halo by shining a flashlight behind the doll's head; there was some difficulty in keeping the flashlight hidden. Then I got to play Joan of Arc. It was an outdoor performance in which I rode a horse to the funeral pyre. Pretty heady stuff. Stardom went right to my head. I joined the drama club and produced and starred in *Billy the Kid*. Then, disastrously, I staged *Pinocchio* wherein I took the parts of both the prevaricator and the Blue Fairy. The performance, dragging on endlessly while I switched and re-switched costumes, was halted by the authorities, much to the relief of the audience. This signaled the end of my career as an actress.

"School days, school days / Dear old golden rules days / Reading and writing and 'rithmetic / Done to the tune of the hick'ry stick . . ." The tune remains, the words are antiquated, but school days—indeed they were golden in many ways.

Part of what made them golden was the general feeling of optimism and idealism almost all of us shared. We were patriotic; the American Revolution and the Civil War seemed quite recent events, not dusty history. When we pledged allegiance to the flag—"with liberty and justice for all"—or sang "My Country 'Tisofthee," our hearts were in the words and we felt proud.

LET'S PRETEND

Let's pretend. How often we did that in our daily play. It seems a bit puzzling that children who are learning so much every day about the real world should be so busy imagining things beyond it. If we climbed a tree, it was more exciting to say we were practicing for a trip to the jungles of Africa where we intended to tame zebras. If we were trying to roast corn or potatoes on a camp fire, why not pretend we were Indians—a bit comic since some of us in fact were. If we were jumping from a barn loft into a pile of hay some twelve feet below, why not imagine that, if we tried hard and believed it enough, we would fly like Peter Pan. We knew perfectly well that we weren't going to Africa, that we couldn't be Indians unless we were born so, that we wouldn't be able to fly. When we picked up too many hints to the contrary, we couldn't continue to believe in Santa Claus but we could pretend to for a time. Then, of course, when we had that I'm-getting-to-be-a-grownup feeling, we would pass on this knowledge to the younger members of the family, shortening their let's pretend time.

We were very fond of fairy stories which were much read aloud and then by ourselves when we could read on our own. The English fairy tales, *The Wonder Clock*, the Brothers Grimm (not, however, Hans Christian Andersen—we did not like his stories). These led to full-blown books of the imagination—

45

Mary Poppins, The Jungle Book, Alice In Wonderland, Pinocchio, The Cuckoo Clock (I liked having the heroine's name), *Water Babies, Wind in the Willows, The Wizard of Oz.* Of course we didn't literally believe these stories but we could pretend; frogs could become handsome princes, witches could almost get you until a good fairy came to your rescue, spells cast on beauteous maidens could be broken, wolves might gobble down dear old grannies. All these tales are so much about the virtues and lack of them, about danger and daring, about loss and finding, right and wrong, good and evil, and always the prospect of a happily-ever-after carrying over into the "real" world, raising our sights and girding, as it were, our loins. Let's pretend.

Some of the adults put logs on the fire of our imaginations. When I left feasts for the fairies in my dollhouse, they would be gone in the morning, a little golden feather dropped on the dollhouse floor, a small bouquet on the table. I knew my father did this, but pretended otherwise—it was the fairies. We kids would make little fairy dinners up in the woods on old tree stumps. It was up to the little people to consume them before the birds and woodland creatures did.

During our family's New York winter stay I had my tonsils out and was quite miserable in bed before and after—one afternoon particularly so. Suddenly a waltz sounded and there on the railing at the foot of my bed a tiny prince and princess danced together, their gossamer wings sparkling. I really knew this had to be the work of my father but for quite a few years I chose to prefer the slim possibility that it was not, treasuring the idea that there had in fact been fairy dancers at the foot of my bed. Then one day in my teens I opened a desk drawer and glimpsed two small, and rather rough-hewn figures. I slammed the drawer shut. I didn't want to see the reality of that long-ago magical happening.

At our grandmother's place in Cooperstown, New York we could look across the lake and see the Brownie Tower, as she called it, a tall stone structure rising just past the water's edge. Our grandmother, big black eyes sparkling, voice hushed, told us that a cranky and reclusive brownie lived there and that we should stay clear of the place. This of course set us to do just the opposite. We'd row across the lake and draw near enough to the brownie's castle so that it would have been possible to see his eyes, if he should be peeking out of one of the slit windows. As we never did see any signs of him, we decided that he slept in the daytime and we'd better not make enough noise to wake him and have to face the wrath that was sure to come down on us.

A summer treat at Cooperstown was Paul Cooper's annual fairy walk in the Brookwood pine woods, which he organized for any children old enough not to get spooked in the dark. He would lead us along, looking for signs of the fairies. Mr. Cooper would point out the various traces—tiny red berries, gossamer threads, miniature ferns—and then, there! There would be the unmistakable sign—a fairy ring, bright little mushrooms in a round. There we would clear a space for a fire, gather kindling, and form a circle for The Ceremony. The little fire would be ablaze and Mr. Cooper would toss some pebble-shaped nuggets into the flames and they would shoot up in brilliant blues and greens, all the colors of the rainbow. And then we had the sparklers! And the marshmallows!

The pine woods were the setting of our childhood's most dramatic presentation. We had sometimes put on plays elsewhere for a restive parental audience, but the performance in the pines was a special triumph, directed by our Uncle Jimmy—playwright and costume designer, as well. I forget the title but it was a Valentinoesque tale about a desert sheik absconding with a beauteous maiden. This part was played by our cousin Suzanne, a beauteous maiden herself, we had to concede, offstage as well as on. Kathie played the Dirty Cook who stirred up the soup in the sheik's tent and kept a watchful eye on the events. There was quite an audience assembled and much laughter and applause.

Everything had gone off without a hitch. Then, just as the final bows were being taken, the grande dame of Cooperstown—she had probably been invited but was making a late arrival—swept in on the scene, her entourage in tow. Uncle Jimmy sent the cast back to repeat the performance. Only this time the Dirty Cook was speechless with stage fright and forgot her lines. Loud prompting from the director to no avail, sent the audience into stitches. Kathie told me that experience made her shy for life.

This dramatic coup led, of course, to a spate of new productions, some staged on the garden house balcony. But none of them were up to the pine woods triumph.

When I was eleven I came on a book of magic recipes in our friends the Chapins' house and purloined it. The pièce de résistance in the book was a recipe for conjuring up fairies before one's very eyes. One would be able to see them, hear them, talk to them. To accomplish this one had to gather the ingredients for a brew to be brought to a boil on a full-moon midnight, then dabbed on one's eyes, ears, mouth. The participants were to sit around the fire built to accommodate the cauldron and wait for the face-to-face meeting with the fairies who would surely come. I enlisted Maria and the two Matthews boys who were visiting the farm at the time. Tommy and Johnny did not hold a high opinion of the proposed enterprise, but decided they'd go along with it to avoid my wrath. "We have to indulge her," Tommy advised a quizzical Johnny. As to the recipe for the magic potion, most of the ingredients were not at hand—juice of pomegranate, eye of newt, dust of antelope horn, edelweiss. Ingenuity prevailed. We plucked petals off marigolds and hollyhocks and mixed them up with a jar of molasses filched from the pantry. We found something, probably an ordinary bucket, to serve as a cauldron. All this was done in a conspiratorial manner—the grownups were not to know. When bedtime came—on the late side since it was summertime's daylight savings time—we all made dummies that would look as if we were asleep in our beds. We trafficked to the bathroom to down the six required glasses of water, my innovation to make up for the lack of the drop of pomegranate juice as per the book's instructions. Finally, with the adults chatting away below in the living room, we snuck down the back stairs, went out past the barns, and down to a meadow area beyond the Owls' house. Then there was much scurrying around to find wood for the fire and little success in getting it going well enough to brew the potion in the bucket. At this point the troops I had dragooned were about to revolt. Mind you, no one had as yet openly criticized the project. But along came David Owl, rifle in hand, ready for action. He thought we were intruders. And then—up on the hilly fields we could see the station wagon's headlights. Our parents were out looking for us. Perhaps they thought we had gone to the creek for a swim since it was such a hot night. We were collected and told no two ways about it to go to bed and behave. The grownups themselves went to bed—it was after midnight. Then the prescribed six glasses of water took effect and there was much tiptoeing—Maria and I from the third floor, the Matthew boys from the second-floor guest room—and whispered meetings in the bathroom. We were all in warm-night nudity clutching our little pillows over our private parts, taking turns at the toilet. The next day no mention was made of the adventure. Who knew whether the absence of pomegranate juice and the other ingredients as well as the unfollowed directives of the recipe caused the failure of the mission. Years later I returned the book to the Chapins, who did not seem to have noticed its absence.

The failed fairy excursion was not as fanciful as another of my let's-pretend games. This one was quite odd, come to think of it. In one of the small back rooms in our house, a pedal organ its only furnishing, hung a picture. It wasn't framed; it seemed to be painted on a slab of cement. It was by an Italian painter, Piero della Francesca I believe; a very strong, calm depiction of soldiers asleep by Christ's tomb. Its presence gave protection against danger, the danger of the nail, a large wrought-iron one in the wall opposite the painting, coming out of the wall. We would pull the window shade down and I would sit at the organ and play ominous chords and rumblings, pedaling furiously, pulling out various stops, changing the dynamics with my knees against the side-wings, my fingers pretty much functioning on their own. Some of the results were odd and eerie indeed. "Concentrate, concentrate." And look! It would seem to all that the nail had moved forward. We were thoroughly scared. Up with the shade! Let's get out of here!

Johnny and Tommy came up with less exotic ideas. We were visiting in Newport at their grandfather Bishop Matthews' place, Boothden. They armed us with shovels and hoes borrowed from the gardener and set us digging tunnels and rooms underground, camouflaging them by putting sod-covered boards over the underground labyrinth. When we got back home we busied ourselves with digging a similar underground hideaway on our lawn. Perhaps the German bombers would mistake the farm for London.

The best tunnel of all was the short-lived, but glorious, blizzard project. One winter there was a real blizzard and so much snow fell that we were completely snowed in on the farm for almost a week. The stretch of road just beyond our front lawn was filled to its bank tops which were a good five or six feet high. The banks were lined with locust trees that our father had planted for their spring aroma. When the blizzard abated we could just as well have been at the Arctic Circle. Bundled up in all the cumbersome winter gear one had to put on in those days, with heavy snow pants, galoshes with buckles (sometimes called arctics), mittens on strings threaded through weighty overcoat arms, scarves, and hats, we were as garb-bloated as astronauts. But what a tunnel we made! We were oblivious to the fact that it all could collapse as we dug deeper and deeper, especially toward the end of the week when the series of sunny days must have been slowly melting the great snow bank. Did our parents know what we were up to? Probably not, just as they didn't know we played touch tag on the high and low beams in the big stone barn.

Boxy was probably my best Let's-Pretend. Kathie and Ben remember the word but not the game. Something had come in a large cardboard box which, emptied of its contents, was left in the toolshed. I gave the box a face and armholes and then, having finished my handiwork, summoned the kids to come and meet the new visitor. They sat outside the toolshed into which I went and donned my disguise, emerging as Boxy, a talkative, jolly creature from some elsewhere place. Boxy liked to be asked questions and to give unexpected answers. Then he would have to leave. Into the toolshed he'd go. Shortly thereafter, out of the toolshed I would come. Kathie and Ben did not put two and two together. Boxy was Boxy, I was Sala (that's what my siblings called me based on Ben's babyhood pronunciation of Griselda). The routine went on for several weeks until one day when the box had been taken away. Kathie and Ben were quite upset over the fact that Boxy had not told them he was going. And I was too.

Secret places. We were always finding them and tantalizing each other. "I'll show you my secret place if . . . " "You can't see my secret place unless . . . " I was quite a one for bossing around my sisters in this way. Well, no bones about it, I was a bossy oldest sister. My youngest sister Kathie, though, once told me something that made me feel a bit better about my domineering streak. She said that yes, I was bossy but I gen-erated fun. And she remembered the little orange monkeys. "The orange monkeys?" "Yes." "What, where . . . ?" "Once you took us to a secret place and showed us the orange monkeys, lots of them, dancing on a bush." "Ah, I remember. Those were blossoms on a weed, the kind you put under water to make the leaves turn silver." "No," Kathie said, "they were little orange monkeys." Let's pretend.

J.O.

At first he was called J.H. Perhaps the H stood for his real father. His mother, Mae, might have been previously married or he could have been born out of wedlock. In any case, he was one of David Owl's family and J.O. was what he came to be called. He was redheaded with freckles to match and pale skinned like his mother. He was shy but called to mind the adage "still waters run deep." He had a very sweet boyish nature.

J.O. and I had a friendship that blossomed and deepened through our working together with the pigeons my father had given me for my eleventh birthday. Mind you, my father wasn't setting up an elaborate pigeon loft, the beginning flock of twenty-four Royal Kings, and the equipment and feed for starters just for the fun of it. This was to be a business enterprise. He took me off to spend two weeks in Duxbury, Massachusetts to learn the ropes there from a Swedish mother-and-daughter team who ran a successful pigeon business selling squabs to fancy restaurants and for private dinner parties. It was a good idea but, like others my father came up with, not entirely practical and rather too early given my age and my school-going. There was a good deal of work involved, not to mention the responsibility, after the first year, for having a financially viable enterprise, me on my own in that department.*

I needed help and J.O. needed to save up for a Boy Scout uniform so that he could go on the troop's trip to Washington, D.C. For the lordly sum of twenty-five cents a week (at the time, half my allowance) J.O. would help me on Saturday mornings with the big weekly pigeon loft cleanup—scraping out the nesting boxes and the droppings on the floor, carrying up more than the usual daily several buckets of water for the baths in the flying pen that overhung the barnyard, getting rid of the mice nests and mice babies.

As we worked together, we began to enjoy each other's company so much that Saturdays became red-letter days. A.B. was extremely jealous and, having a rather lascivious bent, suspicious that we might be "getting up to something." So sometimes we would discover him eavesdropping and peeking down through the ceiling grate and we'd angrily chase him away. What we were "up to" was conversation while we worked. I can't quite imagine what we chatted on about but we talked and talked and came to feel as close as two peas in a pod. We loved each other.

Afternoons when I arrived home from school, J.O. was usually waiting up by our house and, when the weather was warm at night, he would sit under the forsythia bush by the driveway and we would try to whisper—me from my

---

* I struggled with the pigeon business for over three years. I slit the squab throats when they were market-ready, eviscerated them, plucked the feathers, and then they were delivered to the Co-op store in New Hope or to houses where they would be served at parties. The war sent the price of grain and Canadian peas soaring. I struggled to feed the flock and, because of my school hours, could not keep up with the monitoring and record-keeping that needed to be done. It was a sad thing when I had to sell the pigeons off. A hotel in Philadelphia answered my little ad in the *Doylestown Intelligencer* and took the pigeons away in one fell swoop.

third-floor window seat, so one can only think "some whisper-
ing"—back and forth until the parental stricture came down.
We tried communicating with flashlights in Morse Code, but
those conversations were limited indeed. The basic text, noted
down in a 2"x 3" spiral notepad I still have, went as follows:

.--,....,.-,-
.-,.-.,.
-,--,---,..-
-..,---,..,-.--.

"What are you doing?" (a ridiculous question given the
circumstances).
"Where is Darleena?"
"I love you."
"I am going to sleep now" (obviously prepared for the
parental stricture to come down).

Generally after the dit-dotting a loud "What did you say?"
would ensue. Darleena, our Hermes, would trip back and forth
between houses to inform us how things were on the homefront. Was David about to come and fetch J.O.? Was A.B. on a
spying trip, lurking around somewhere?

One August night when the kids and I were sleeping in the
playhouse by the barnyard—the building that had a pigpen on
the lower level and the upper used for spreading walnuts out to
dry—as I dangled my arm out the window, suddenly J.O. was
there below. He took my hand in his. No words. Once in a while
we had wrestled around but this was a new intimacy. Later my
sister Maria, who followed the romance with great interest, con-
fessed that she too had held J.O.'s other hand for a while.

I was so thrilled I thought I would never get to sleep but I drifted off to the sound of the sleeping sheep and the August insects, under the Milky Way sky, J.O.'s warm hand in mine. When dawn broke and the barnyard stirrings woke me up, J.O. was still there, my hand still in his. Then David came along to do the morning chores and, discovering J.O., took him off by the scruff of his neck. Darleena reported that her father had given him a whale of a whipping with a belt. It took J.O. quite a few days to regain his spirits.

Eventually, one can only suppose, we would have "gotten up to something." But that would have been a ways down the line. It was A.B.'s lascivious nature that brought our day-to-day relationship to an end.

What happened was this. Every now and then David and whatever young or older men were around—there often being someone up from the Cherokee reservation staying in the Owls' house or in the barn lofts—would go off on a trip to Trenton. They would drink, probably visit prostitutes, and definitely, A.B. was sure to tell us, put quarters in the peep machines. "Nec-ked bodies," A.B. informed us. J.O., being fourteen, had finally been deemed old enough to join the grownups and go on a trip to Trenton. The next day Darleena reported the state of affairs. J.O. had gotten drunk and was still drunk. I met him on the road halfway between the houses to see for myself. There he was—drunk as a lord, wobbly on his feet, bleary-eyed, his speech slurred and incoherent. I was disturbed. A prudish strain came out. Off I stormed.

I was working off my upset, furiously weeding a row of vegetables in the garden, when Darleena came to bring the message that J.O. was waiting to apologize. Could I meet him in the barnyard? A weight lifted from my heart. I trotted down to the barnyard. What I found was J.O., of course still drunk, and with him A.B. J.O. had not a word to say. He stood red-faced and miserable. But A.B., with evident delight—now I gotcha—told me that J.O. wanted to "put his thing in me" or equally unseemly words to that effect. I was appalled. But mostly I was wounded to the core that J.O. had let A.B., both behind my back and now, into our private world. And too, my prudery and pride took over. I could not forgive him, especially not there and then. Later the faithful messenger Darleena was dispatched to tell J.O. that I was never going to speak to him again.

A few miserable days passed. I cried my heart out; Maria being solicitous, sharing the Kleenexes. I had not seen J.O. at

J.O.

all and then as I was coming out of the pigeon loft, there he was. The tears streamed down his face. He pleaded to be forgiven. I couldn't bring myself to do so.

That was not, however, the end of this love story. After the parting of ways we kept clear of each other. Time passed. In due course I went off to boarding school; J.O. went off to the navy and the Pacific. I saw him only one more time. That was when he was discharged from the navy—and married. It was an awkward encounter.

Some thirty years later I got word that J.O. was dying of cancer. I wrote him to say I had never forgotten our times together and loved him still.

That seemed to be that. But it was not the end of the love story. A good year after J.O.'s death I got a phone call from my stepmother, who had been enjoined by Darleena and her husband Shaler to convey a deathbed message to me. They had procrastinated over conveying it because they didn't feel comfortable about hurting J.O.'s family even if unbeknownst to them. But Shaler had given his word, so I received the message. J.O. wanted me to know that throughout his life he loved me most of all. He was very happy when he got my letter. "Who's that from?" his son asked. "It's from the person who might have been your mother," J.O. answered. Heart's treasures we were to each other. Sometimes I think of it and am back under the August Milky Way sky on the night through which J.O. held my hand.

He is buried in the same little country graveyard near Wabasso, Florida in the company of David Owl and my father.

MOSTLY ABOUT ANIMALS

Probably nothing else in our childhood was from day to day more interesting than the outdoors—"Can I go outdoors now?" a frequent query. There would be some strictures about what to put on beforehand—in winter a cumbersome load, strings on mittens, buckles on galoshes (our arctics). Or what not to take off on a warm early spring day, our shoes and the hated winter undershirts. Otherwise Ma, who kept track of our goings in and out, was happy to give us the green light.

Outdoors, whatever we might be up to, we still took note of things: the orioles starting to repair their nest in the tree where the swing was or the perfume of the locust trees in bloom along our road, or an emerald-green beetle spotted under a leaf—"Look! Look! See what I found," or milkweed pods ready to set their white silk-festooned seeds flying, or a new butterfly to net for my collection—"Damn, damn, it's getting away!"

We were always on the lookout for the "wild" animals, that is, those gentle untamed creatures of the Pennsylvania woods—rabbits, squirrels, chipmunks, groundhogs, deer. In our view these animals weren't wild, they were simply very shy. If we could stand still long enough, speak calmly enough, move towards them slowly enough, they would become pets. We felt sure of this because now and then we would take care of a baby wild thing and it would become tame: Ben's squirrel

Nutkin, for instance. Nutkin would come down from the trees when called and he was perfectly at home inside the house. Indeed, Nutkin's fearlessness led to his death. He drowned in the toilet. He must have been trying to get a drink of water.

We seemed to be used to pets dying or just not being around anymore. Some of them must have been quietly taken away by our parents like, for instance, our first family dog, a gray-and-white shaggy English sheep dog, Whiskey. He was by temperament the ideal dog for children. He was perfectly amenable to having his ears and tail pulled, to being sat on or used as a punching bag. He was around for quite a few years (I think only Ben was too young to remember him now.) Yet I don't think there was any to-do about Whiskey's death, certainly nothing like the ceremonial funeral for Peanuts. He just wasn't around anymore.

For me, the death of my pet lamb Yamie was a very sad blow. He was run over by Tom Matthews, who had come on a hasty visit to check out the arrangements for the imminent arrival of the people who were coming to stay on the farm. Tom was in a rush and did not check under his car before starting off; he usually would have, since dogs and other animals often hunkered down under parked cars on warm days. We always checked before starting off. Tom tracked me down to tell me about the accident. I was speechless. I dashed off to the organ room, pulled down the shades—"Leave me alone!"—and spent the rest of the afternoon playing dirge-like inventions through a stream of tears.

Yamie, one of twins, had been rejected by his mother and I had raised him on a bottle. He grew only a smidgen bigger than he had been at birth. He was the "author" of *Yamie: A Lamb's*

Tale, one of my proudest literary achievements at that point, and he had been the most faithful of companions. I did not want to see his little dead body and I never asked who buried it and where.

With the exceptions of the cat Jereboam, the parrot Miranda, the pig Benjamin, and Ben's turtle called Fluff, our pets were dogs. Cats were relegated to the barns and when a litter of kittens came, it was usually put, along with a few stones, into a burlap sack and taken down to the pond. Jereboam somehow escaped that fate. He was absolutely pink in color and very large and he won his, to us, knightly name (it must have been given when the Bible was being read aloud) for his prowess in battles with groundhogs. He also may have been the reason my nest of robins came a cropper.

I don't recall how I came by them, but one spring I had four fledgling robins to care for. They were almost ready to fly and they were constantly and ravenously hungry. I had everyone digging for worms, especially Jean Shook and Ria, who were experts because of their fishing expeditions. Feeding the birds took over the daytime. Then they began to get hungry in the night. One night they chirped so much I simply could not get to sleep, so I took the nest down to the kitchen wing and left it in the pantry. The next morning, not a feather remained. Jereboam looked especially pleased with himself. I think he finally met his fate in the field of battle with a groundhog.

I had better luck with ducks. Bousie, knowing the ducks' eggs were about to hatch, brought me three, and told me to keep them warm in my lap. So there I sat on the lawn outside the kitchen not knowing what to expect. Before I got thoroughly restive, things began to happen. The ducklings were pecking their way out into the world. In hardly any time at all, I became the three duckling's mother, that's how they regarded me. They were named Tommy, Johnny, and Paul after the Matthews boys. We would lead them down to the pond and encourage them about life on the water. We could not pack up ducks for the summer trip to Cooperstown and when we returned, they were gone.

The farm had the usual assortment of farm animals—pigs, cows (eventually just one, our almost-a-pet, Sally), poultry, but of most importance there was the flock of sheep, I think several hundred in number. There was a pattern to the flock's year, commencing with the ram's visit in early fall. I don't think we ever had our own ram; Bousie hired a different one each year. One time the ovine lothario spent some time penned up behind our house. We viewed him with suspicion, wondering if he was going to measure up to the task. Not only did his male equipment dangle down but he had a leaky bladder; there was a steady dribble. Appearances, however, proved to be misleading—his was the year when an unusual number of twin births occurred.

The lambing season signaled that winter was truly over. Once the lambs started coming, they came thick and fast. There were always some sad disasters. Sometimes a mother sheep would die, leaving an orphan. Bousie and David would try to entice another ewe to adopt, but that was a difficult task so some orphans had to be bottlefed. If they connected too closely with humans, they were shunned when put back into the flock. There was one orphan we called Tessie who wanted to keep being peoplefriendly while at the same time fit in with the other sheep. She was never accepted. If she drew near the flock, she was butted aside.

Thinking of the sheep brings to mind the Scottish sheep dog, Ring. Bousie told us that Ring was not a pet because he was to become a working sheep dog. This posed problems. Poor Ring was consigned to being tied up in the big barn most of the time. And, of course, we petted him. And, of course, he barked a lot hoping we would let him loose. Then Bousie would take him for a training session and, I regret to say, those generally did not go well. Ring did not learn much; perhaps better said, did not take to learning much about filling his professional dogly duties, and Bousie was not a patient trainer. He gave up on the project after he realized he was losing his temper and that would get them nowhere. Sad to say, Ring took to wandering. He left our sheep alone but he crossed over to the other side of Jericho Mountain and became a sheep-killer there. Finally he was shot in the woods by one of the farmers who had caught him red-handed.

Soon after they are born, lambs begin to show their frolicsome character, delightful and endearing to see. Capricious and joyful, they are still very obedient about answering their mother's summons. The barnyard is filled with baaing and maaing sounds. Then, one day, along comes the truck that will take the lambs. After it leaves, there is a cacophony of baaing from the bereaved mothers. It takes the ewes a while to realize that their lambs are gone and to forget them.

Not long after this, it's time for the shearers. There would be several. They worked with wonderful speed, almost as if racing against each other, as perhaps they were. They could often shear off a sheep's entire coat in one piece. The wool would be stuffed into huge burlap bags which were weighed before being put on the shearer's truck. Poor sheep, they would seem mortified by their new nakedness and they weren't a pretty sight, especially if they had a dark salve on various nicks and cuts. In this rather abject state, they would have to endure being shoved through the sheep dip. But then, it was off to fresh pasture, their wool coatings began to grow back, and in a few months' time the cycle of their sheep-year started all over again.

Of all the animal events we experienced, the most dramatic was the rabid-dog happening. It was strikingly similar to the one later filmed in *To Kill a Mockingbird*. A spring day afternoon, we are on the front porch. Coming towards us up across the lawn, wobbly, drooling, head hanging, a large, shaggy brown dog we do not know. We can tell he is dangerous. There's Bousie with his shotgun (I never saw where he kept his guns—he had several). He's taking aim, he's firing, he has shot the mad dog squarely in the middle of his forehead. The dog stops dead in his track and falls. For a while afterwards his menace seemed to linger on the front lawn. And our father—how could we have admired him more!

It seems to me now that the story of our pets is one of loss connected with degrees of lasting affection. And sometimes all but forgotten. *The Jackson Quarterly* news column for the summer of 1939 notes that "the children have been given a puppy named Lucky." None of us remembers Lucky beyond the name. I think, at the time, we had too much else on our minds.

DOING THE RIGHT THING

We were, by and large, well-behaved children but of course we were sometimes quarrelsome, sometimes mischievous, and sometimes just plain naughty. When those sometimes came up, we got admonished or punished accordingly, no pussy-footing about paying the piper.

Our mother was our teacher in regard to manners. How to behave at table and in the company of grownups, how to shake hands and make a little curtsy with a bend of the knee—a habit I was still trying to break in my early twenties. And there was saying "please" and "thank you" and, when old enough, writing thank-you notes for Christmas and birthday presents. These small mannerly things, we were taught, mattered.

Bousie was the judge and administrator of justice. Tops on the list of offenses was telling a lie; he considered this the worst of sins. Get caught telling one and out came the brown soap to wash out your mouth. We never got slapped but sometimes we got spanked. That could be a quick whomp on the bottom or a more formal affair—approach the judge, bend over his knee, and then some whacks with hand or hairbrush depending on the severity of the crime. Occasionally we were made to stand in the corner in the front hall for what would seem like endless minutes. Sometimes it was "Go to your room," term of incarceration depending on the gravity of the offence. Being sent to one's room always seemed at first like an easy penalty, but the sense of disgrace would begin to weigh and then, what was everyone else up to? They were probably having a great time while you were feeling sorry for yourself and getting bored. Usually the hardest part of any of the punishments was falling out of Bousie's grace.

There were two punishments meted out to me that I especially remember because I thought they were unjust. In the first of them I was showing off, using a "big" word—I wish I could recall it—that I'd picked up from whatever book I was reading at the time. "You can't use that word in that way. You don't know what the word means," Bousie said. "I know what it means to me," says Miss Smartypants. Whereupon the judge, who knew more about words and their meanings than anyone else I've ever met, sprang up, grabbed me out of my seat at the breakfast table, and whomped me hard on the butt. Was that for the misused word or the sass? In front of everyone! My mother demurred, a rare thing. What was the *word*, though? I still wonder.

The other occasion was quite different. I was sent to my room for the day on bread and water. I felt righteous indignation for I was sure I had not done whatever it was I was being punished for. I refused the bread and water that Pauline brought up on a tray at noontime, and nourished myself on my outrage. Bored and no less miffed as the afternoon wore on, I began singing out my bedroom window about the injustice and I did not hold my tongue. Suddenly, there he was standing below and summoning me—"Come down *now!*" Had I not been singing that my father was unfair and I hated him? But he made no reference to my song or the day on bread and water. Instead, he said "Look what I found when I was plowing," and there was a baby rabbit. He must have realized that I hadn't done whatever he'd sent me to prison for. I was touched to the core.

We raised the little animal. He grew into a very large, handsome rabbit and a fine pet. He traveled up on the train with us for the summer Cooperstown visit. One evening there was a grownup party in the garden. Our Uncle Jimmy, probably fortified with party punch, released our rabbit, to our great disapproval when we discovered the empty cage the next day. Calling the bunny—he had a name, of course, but I've forgotten it—did not bring him hopping back. Though he had been perfectly tame, once out on his own he forgot all about us.

Stories we heard and observing the ways of people we knew gave us many clues about good manners and doing the right thing. And we figured things out about them on our own as well.

I remember recognizing that I was being naughty. I had a pair of scissors and time on my hands. So I busily set to clipping off the plush of an F.A.O. Schwartz elephant-on-wheels and then, enjoying myself, cutting off all my teddy bear's hair. He remained beloved even though naked and a reminder of what it felt like to be naughty.

But there were several more serious not-doing-the-right-things that I don't particularly enjoy remembering. Hurting someone's feelings was something I learned about when our family was living in a New York apartment one winter. We had an Irish au pair. She was a very young girl and, it is my surmise, had only recently arrived from Ireland. I was quite sick for a stretch and miserable, recovering from a tonsillectomy. One day this girl brought me a present, "To cheer you up," she said. A coloring book, I think it was. Instead of being appreciative, I was so wrapped up in how badly I felt that I snapped at her and told her to go away and leave me alone. She disappeared into the adjoining bathroom and soon I heard her sobbing as if her heart would break. Probably it wasn't all on my account, but I knew I was in some way responsible. What a feeling of being sorry swept over me. I wanted to make it up to her. I tried, but saying "I'm sorry" didn't really do the trick. I learned that what is done and said cannot be undone and unsaid. Shortly after this incident the Irish girl left our employ and when she did I knew I really hadn't made things right.

And then, there was a case of mindless cruelty on my part. I can see myself—probably I am around nine years old. I'm on the pond's dock and I have caught a frog and there's a stone in my hand and I am bashing the frog's head. Then in a flash, just as I had comprehended the Irish girl's sobs and what it meant to hurt someone's feelings, I am horrified at myself and, because I certainly knew better, ashamed. To this day I can recall the incident as though it just happened.

Brown soap in the mouth, standing in the corner, getting whomped on the bottom, feeling sorry or guilty about something I had done; the punishments received were not frequent but they seemed to me to be part of the adventure of life, food for thought, and small, vivid dramas about doing the right thing.

READING AND WRITING

Books were a living presence in our lives. They lived in book-cases in the two big downstairs rooms and in each of our bed-rooms; they sat on bed tables and window sills. Sometimes they came wrapped in holiday or birthday paper. They were for taking down, opening up, looking at, listening to, and, one day, being able to read all by oneself. It always strikes me that something is missing if a home is without books.

As we grew older we "borrowed" books from the down-stairs shelves, often books that were quite beyond our grasp. Back they went for a later time or sometimes I would slog through a book without a clue. *Sons and Lovers* made no sense to a twelve-year-old. *The Sun Also Rises* was easier to comprehend, at least minimally.

And there were some volumes good for a rainy afternoon—those filled with pictures, introducing us to art. But at first, of course, books were for being read aloud, a before-bedtime practice that continued as we graduated from children's books with lots of pictures to ever more sophisticated ones.

We had our prejudices. *Treasure Island* was never finished because we thought it was a copout that the castaways could return to the shipwreck and find almost everything they needed. And our mother had to give up on *The Pickwick Papers*. She found it hilarious, but we got bored. And, speaking of getting bored, I can't imagine how Kathie and Ben sat through *Barchester Towers*.

And then it was *Huckleberry Finn, Lorna Doone, David Copperfield, The Black Arrow*. One doesn't forget the illustrations in many childhood books—the Beatrix Potters, the N.C. Wyeths, Rackhams, Howard Pyles, and many whose names were not remembered but whose drawings and paintings still are: the wonderfully Renoiresque painting of Rose White and Rose Red, the princess seeing her fairy godmother on the castle roof, Toad and his friends, the simple little black-and-white drawings in *The English Fairy Tales*, and countless others. Illustrations put their stamp on the stories so that, for instance, when I saw *The Wizard of Oz* it just didn't seem to me that it had the right Dorothy, Scarecrow, Tin Woodsman, and Cowardly Lion.

One year it was the Bible in the morning before breakfast, from the Old Testament through the New. This reading project ended dramatically. When we got to the crucifixion, Bousie became very emotional. It was, as far as I can remember, the only time I saw him cry.

"Oh, please—one more chapter" transferred to one's private reading. "Turn out your light *now*." Ah, the discovery of the usefulness of a flashlight under the covers!

I was keen on learning to read by myself, and early on helped by the Calvert System of home instruction. Years later Tom Matthews told me that there had been a contest between my father and him, both armed with Calvert, as to whether I or his son Tommy would be the first to read. At some point Tom asked me how the lessons were going and I said "Oh, we don't do them anymore." "Why?" "Because we fight too much."

I don't recall the fighting, but still can visualize the tidy little primers—much more appealing than the Dick and Jane books of elementary school—and the beautiful letters that could be rotated to spell out words—*cat, bag, get, did* would become *eat, beg, bet, dad*. Then one could add letters—*scat, cabbage, forget, didn't*—though I don't think we got beyond three-letter words. Maybe that was when we started to fight. In any case I did learn how to read and write well before school-going came along.

Writing was almost as interesting to me as reading. It started off with letters:

(Dec. 1933)

Dear Mr. Harper
i am Glad you sent
my RaBBit's tail home to me.
MARiA and KAthARiNe are Very
well. Give my love to Mrs.
HaRper.
my fatherhas a cold
I hoPe yoare WeLL
Goodby
from Griselda
WRite me

And write me Mr. Harper did for many years. Here are two irresistible early examples:

March 17, 1935
(on Regent Palace Hotel, Picadilly stationery)

Dear Griselda,

Your lovely letter came several days ago and made me very happy. It is a great thing to be able to write so nice a letter, and worth going to school through snow and mud. Here we have really not seen winter at all. Daisies, crocuses, daffodils, forsythia, and other flowers and blossoms have been blooming for weeks and weeks. One day recently we saw the King of England, George the Fifth. He was in a gilt coach drawn by handsome horses, with a grand coachman sitting on the box in front and two gorgeous footmen behind. On the top of the coach was a large crown to distinguish it from others, of which there were several. Soldiers on horseback and a band of music went before. The King is a nice looking man. He did not recognize me in the crowd and therefore did not wave his hand at me. If I had shouted "I am a friend of Griselda & Maria & their sister Katherine & their brother with blue eyes," of course he would have spoken to us and maybe asked us to get into the coach beside him. I hope you are planting flowers and vegetables. It is such fun to watch them growing. I once knew a big girl who had a garden of which she was proud. She asked me to go and see her planting onions. And what do you suppose she did? She stuck them in the ground (I mean the little seed onions) upside down. If I hadn't laughed, perhaps they would have grown downward and come out in China, which is on the other side of the Earth. [here there is a charming drawing] Please tell your Daddy and Mamma that we have had to lunch with a great granddaughter of Samuel Taylor Coleridge. That made up for not being invited to ride in the King's coach. Here are a few kisses

XXXXXXXXXXXXXXXXXXXXXXXXXXXXXX
We expect to go home to America early in May.
Much love to you all – Yours affectionately,
George M. Harper

And here's another letter I can't resist including:

Dear Griselda: Feb.15,1938

Won't you please help me to solve an important and puzzling problem? Your mind is probably more active than mine. I am a slow-coach, as is shown by the fact that I postponed sending any valentines till it was too late—even to my own daughter, daughter-in-law, and grand-daughters. You see, Sunday came just the day before, & I had forgotten about that.

Well, the problem is about a valentine. It is this: I received this morning a very pretty one, in the shape of a red heart, with small hearts here & there all over it. The post-mark on the envelope was NEW HOPE, PA., and that is why I turn to you for help. There are few people I know in or near New Hope except you and your family, but there is a whole school of young ladies there, and artists, and one or two persons who try to write books, and I can't imagine which one of them would be sending me a valentine. You live so near New Hope that perhaps you can give me your opinion in this matter. Perhaps you can find out if there is any lady in or near New Hope foolish enough to send a valentine to an old fellow like me. If she is as pretty and sweet as her valentine, it would be a shame for me not to make her acquaintance. My idea is as follows: Some girl friend of yours, who lives at or near New Hope, has heard you say that you have a dear friend in Princeton named George M. Harper, and the poor child, having no boy friend of her own, just caught at the name and sent me her valentine because she couldn't think of anybody else & had confidence in your judgement. Here's a story about Mary McLean: Her father took her to one of his lectures at Williams College and gave her a seat in the front row, with a pencil & sheet of paper to take notes. She sat very quietly all through the lecture. Next day, however, she was heard to say, "I've decided not to go to college." But being a kind little girl & fond of her father, she said to him on the <u>following</u> day: "Daddy, you are a good teacher."

Please give my dear love to your Father & Mother & Maria & Katherine & little Schuyler, & tell the Owls I remember them with pleasure. And don't show this letter to that New Hope girl!

Your loving friend,

George M. Harper

Mr. Harper was like a member of the family. My other two childhood correspondents, however, were gentlemen friends I made on my own. Between the three of them and some mail from an aunt or a grandma or my father when he was away for a bit, I developed a great interest in going to pick up the mail. Our mailbox was a mile down the dirt road leading to Brownsburg, on the River Road. Brownsburg consisted of at most a dozen houses with a one-room schoolhouse on its outskirts where the Owl children went until it closed and they were bused elsewhere. Mrs. Billings and Pauline Allen, both of whom did work for us, lived in Brownsburg. Its only commercial enterprise was a candy counter in the front room of a house that reeked of cats, so much so that it was not a place to linger when we occasionally went in to spend a few pennies on a bag of chocolate-covered malted-milk balls. The place could hardly be considered even a village yet all that we needed as an address was simply Brownsburg, Pa. Later the address got upgraded to a simple New Hope, Pa., New Hope being some seven miles up the River Road. And the mail was delivered rain or shine. One would never walk down to get it and have to cool one's heels waiting—mail was always there by noontime. When you picked it up, you raised the mailbox flag and left the letters that the mailman was to collect on the way back from his rounds. My enthusiasm for walking down to Brownsburg to pick up the mail grew as my correspondence did. It was always very pleasant on the walk back if one had a letter. One did not open any mail until one was home again.

Sometimes it was very hard to resist opening a letter before getting back home–like waiting for warm tapwater to turn cool before quenching an urgent thirst. My greatest test in waiting to open a letter, to jump ahead in time a little, was an envelope addressed by hand, on the back flap the name and address of Roddy McDowall. I had fallen in love with *How Green Was My Valley*—and of course with Roddy too, and had written a letter, and here was an answer! Trot, run, get home as fast as you can! It turned out that we would exchange letters throughout our teens before drifting away in our very different worlds. It was quite an adventure when we finally met, but that belongs in another tale.

My other two early pen pals initiated our correspondence to each other. The first of these was Mr. Gareis. In retrospect I realize he must have come to the U.S. to escape Hitler's Germany. He owned a house in New York City, one just off Fifth Avenue in the forties, and he rented out rooms. My father stayed there weekdays for a time in 1935 when he had some sort of job—I think it was at *Fortune*—and one day my mother took me along on a trip to town. She left me for the afternoon in Mr. Gareis's care. I had a lovely time with him, he was a sweet host, and shortly after that visit, this letter arrived:

Sunday before Easter 1935.
Dear little friend Griselda:

When you were in my yard the other day, I showed you that hole in the wire fence, do you remember? Now imagine what has happened! Easter-Bunny, calling at this time of the year on gardens and yards of houses in which good children are supposed to be, really came through this hole in the fence and left three Easter eggs in the shrubbery in the rear—you know at the right-hand side of that board fence where a knot hole is in the middle board; we two looked over through this hole in the other yard which is a children's playground and we saw some kids playing in the sand and their nurses sitting at the wall; then we threw some little toys they had stuffed through that knothole over to our yard, back again to their yard, because they might still like to play with them. Now just to the right of that place was the spot, where the three eggs were found.

I wonder how Bunny had found out about you and your

two sisters, because there is no child in my house, except you, when dear Mama brings you along to the City; maybe he was just hiding in the big park next to my yard and saw you & heard you telling me about your two sisters.

I am so glad that your dear Papa is living here, so I can request him to bring this parcel out to you next weekend, that saves me going to the Post Office, to inquire, as I do not know much about rules, to send Easter eggs by mail. Do not fail please to ask dear Mama for permission to see me when in N.Y. again, because I am your friend, Gareis.

Every Christmas Mr. Gareis would send me a box of Speculatins, a German Christmas cookie, and I would send him some imperfectly realized fudge. In 1939 he wrote: "the package is very small this year, you know, the English don't want American children to eat German Speculatins, so they take it from ships, if they find it. Well, this time will pass by too, and we will be able to eat in America all the German cookies we want."

My correspondence with Mr. Gareis lasted until his death in 1940. I had sent him the usual fudge for Christmas and soon received the following in the mail, a letter which introduced me to the idea of people dying. I was startled and sad. But only for a while. Then the callowness of youth put thoughts of Mr. Gareis aside. Only when I was older did I fully appreciate him and my two other faithful gentlemen correspondents.

Jan 24, 1941
Miss Griselda Jackson,

Many thanks for the wonderful fudge you sent to Mr, Gareis. He could not write you himself, as he had to go to the hospital, being ill since quite some time. Indeed he had trouble with his heart for such a long time that he told me repeatedly he wouldn't mind if he would die, as this would be

rather a release for him. —I'm the fellow who takes care of
the house during his helplessness; other people didn't suspect how seriously ill he was. —So he died peacefully and
without pains, beginning of December after having lived
long and gracefully, and having made real friends, like you
for instance. GOD will bless you for your good heart, —and
good fudge.
With friendly regards,
Joseph Stohr

My third correspondent was Alfred Yeomans—he picked
me up. I was ten years old and staying at my grandmother's
winter house in Southern Pines, North Carolina. My parents
had left me there for the spring term—I believe because Maria
had been dangerously ill and, after taking her on a recupera-
tive trip to Jamaica, they thought it best to have me out of the
way while she was being nursed back to health. I was enrolled
to attend The Ark, a private girl's school that, having no boarders at the time, took day pupils. I was destined to be the only
boarder when the term began. Meanwhile I had a stretch on
my own at my grandmother's.

Near her house there was a large lot filled with sand and
here I began laying out a Babar sort of city. I was much occupied with this project and one day along came Mr. Yeomans
who had spotted my grand city and became curious to see the
architect and landscape artist responsible for it (he was himself an architect). This is what he wrote about our first meeting
some years later in our frequent exchange of letters:

> I still walk past there on my afternoon strolls and never
> without thinking of you—a small girl in a sweater just like
> the one in your picture—laying out your model village. I
> remember too that your grandmother didn't like it any too
> much when we went for a walk without letting her know.

I didn't blame her either—she must have thought you had been kidnapped."

Our letter writing started when The Ark opened. I was into codes and picturalizing, Mr. Yeomans replying in kind. But here is an uncoded one from him, albeit in French, at that point, something of a code to me—I was having a beginners French class in school:

Chere Mlle Jackson:

Si vous insistez de m'appeller "Monsieur Y." Naturellerment il me faut vous appeller "Mlle J." Mais je n'aime pas ça. J'aime beaucoup mieux "Alfred" or "Alf" comme vous écrit autrefois. Et pourquois pas? Nous sommes des bons amis n'est-ce-pas? Nous aimons les mêmes choses—jouer de piano ou de violin, promener á la campagne, battir les petites villes, parler de tout chose dans le monde. Alors, ne m'appellez pas Monsieur Y. s'il vous plait.
J'espère que les deux petits cochons se trouvent bien. Peut être ils iront promener avec nous un jour. Je pense ça ferait plaisir pour eux. Il faut etre tres ennuyent rester toujours dans leur petit jardin—sans fleurs, sans amis, sans tout. Ne pensez vous pas?
Adieu ma chère Mille Jackson. J'espère de vous voir Vendredi a la fête, n'est ce pas?
Il y a beaucoup de fautes dans cette lettre mais si vous ne comprenez tout je vous assisterai Vendredi.
Au revoir,

Alfred

Mr. Yeomans was a quintessential southern bachelor gentleman. He lived with his two unmarried sisters. It was a lively household; it was apparent that they got on splendidly with each other. They were all good amateur musicians and played together as well as with their friends of a similar bent. They read a lot and kept up with the times—national politics and world events engrossed them. Their views on race evolved so that, in Mr. Yeomans's case at least, though he was disturbed somewhat by the fact that my one-room-schoolhouse classmate Charlie was "colored," he gradually accepted such ideas and came to believe what our Declaration of Independence says about the equality of all men.

On the weekends, Mr. Yeomans often took me home for tea and I would fill up on home-baked cookies and cakes and be treated with a kind of formal courtliness like quite a grownup visitor. Sometimes they picked an easy piece and I played the piano along with their string instruments. And he and I would frequently take a walk and retrace the steps of our first acquaintance.

I only saw Mr. Yeomans in person once more after the stay in Southern Pines. Unfortunately it was not a successful encounter. I had no idea he was going to be dropping by. I was in school where we were getting ready for the Christmas party. Charlie was to be Santa and we were filling his sack with the presents—those each of us was supposed to bring, along with Mrs. Leedom's, purchased by her, as were many other things, out of her own pocket. Mr. Yeomans, on his way to New York, had stopped by the farm. How he found it beats me. My mother offered to escort him over Jericho Mountain to the one-room schoolhouse. Called out, I stood embarrassed, speechless. I can't fathom why, but in any case it was a great disappointment to my gentleman caller, so much so that he telegraphed me from New York to say so, adding that he loved me nonetheless and always would. I was rather too young for this dramatic missive, as Mr. Yeomans quickly realized might be the case. I tore up the telegram. He wrote to apologize and better explain himself. It was a definite hump we had to get over but get over it we did. Yet, afterwards, I always felt a little sad about him because I sensed that in the back of his mind he would always feel badly that I had treated him more like a stranger than a fond friend. The subject came up every now and then. In any case, our correspondence continued for almost fifteen more years until his death. That left me with a sore spot because I had owed him a letter for quite a few months and now I couldn't make it up, this adding to my regret that we did not meet again and expunge, as surely we would have, the traces of the meeting outside my school house.

Mr. Harper, Mr. Gareis, and Mr. Yeomans—my three gentlemen as I thought of them and still do—became the first subscribers to my principal literary endeavor. This was *The Jackson Weekly* established in 1936. This magazine quickly turned into *The Jackson Monthly*. The editor G.A.B.C.* Jackson, always referring to herself as "he" (but, let me say parenthetically, with no feeling of inferiority about being "she"), made the decision that even monthly would not work, so the title became *The Jackson Quarterly* until, at Mr. Yeoman's suggestion, it settled on its final name—*The Jackson Quarterly Appearing at Irregular Intervals*. This was a perfect solution. Over the course of the four -year lifetime of this ambitious project the subscription rate soared from a nickel to a quarter and the subscribers from one to eight.

* A for Atlee, B for Brinckerhoff, C for Cenerentola

The front page of my magazine carried the news, much concerned with the doings on the farm. The final issue, which was especially elaborate, had headlines **OLD NEWS OF THE PAST MONTHS** followed by a fresh section, **NEWS. NEW NEWS.** The most dramatic news page appeared in the fall, 1939 number, for reference was made to the fateful summer events, though the reader would hardly suspect how traumatic they had been.

In addition to the news, there were stories, poems, puzzles, or riddles (often cribbed), contributions from the subscribers and, in the last issues, from Maria and Kathie. The magazine was filled with illustrative material. At first Crayolas' supplied color. Then Mongol pencils came along and then watercolor.

In the early issues everything was hand written—carbon paper came in very handy. Then one day, as Bousie and I were driving along the River Road, I spotted two swans. "Nonsense," said Bousie, but he slowed down and pulled over. Indeed there were two swans on the river. He said he would think of a reward for my beady eyes. The reward turned out to be a typewriter with an all-capital-letter font. Later I acquired an old Underwood.

In addition to my magazine, I wrote poems and children's stories, all quite derivative from the books I'd read or those being read aloud. All of us considered story writing and picture making fun and worthwhile doing. After all, we knew our father was a writer and we were familiar with other writers as well as some artists.

I sent off my Yamie story to several publishing companies and learned about rejection letters—nice but no. My one literary triumph was winning a first-prize slot in The Pennsylvania Farmer's contest for an essay on "What Home Means to Me."

This was a real thrill. I had forgotten all about sending in my piece—months had passed. I was in bed with the measles when the letter came along with a copy of the magazine with my essay printed in it and a check for the five dollar prize. The room was darkened with the window shades down, but one can be sure I read this mail.

Me and Ma

Me and the family

Bousie

Me and Maria

Ma

The Big House, 2001

OTHER PEOPLE—OTHER PLACES

How many, many times we popped into the car to go the seven miles to New Hope accompanying our mother headed for the A&P! Now New Hope is a congested, touristy place: then, it was just a small village. It had a railroad station nonetheless from which one could journey to Philadelphia, Willow Grove, where there was an amusement park, and, with a transfer, get to Atlantic City. Just about any shopping one needed to do could be done on one short stretch of Main Street. There the most imposing building was the bank—a place where a savings account could be started with a dollar and earn interest even if further deposits were few and far between. When I closed out my account after a dozen years or so, the grand total was in the neighborhood of $10.08. Catty-corner to the bank was Benny Sidon's drugstore, which was also stocked with all sorts of nonpharmaceuticals—tempting candy bars and bubble gum (my brother confessed to some thievery in this department), books, clocks, gloves, the makings of ice- cream cones, sodas, and sundaes. Down the street were Cryer's Hardware Store, the A&P, and a fledgling Co-op. There was a dentist (we went instead to one in Princeton) and two doctor's homes/offices on this part of Main Street. Dr. Leiby's large white house was there though we rarely went, as he made housecalls when his patients were sick in bed. Slightly beyond this "commercial" stretch was The Craft Shop, a place we went to before Christmas to find special presents. I believe it is still there.

In those days most people who owned businesses had their homes in the same place as their work, often above their stores. Beyond The Craft Shop it was all residential. We knew some who lived in this part of town: the frame maker Paul Badura, the painter Jack Folinsbee, one of a number of distinguished artists living then in Bucks County, and a seamstress whose name escapes me but to whom we were taken several times a year to have school and play clothes made. Oh, how long the time seemed standing still while a hem was pinned up or an armhole adjusted. I'm sure my sisters and I will never forget the shorts she made in a style copied from those some cousins had worn while attending school in Switzerland. These shorts—blue with orange stripes at the sides, or white with red—constituted our basic everyday warm-weather play clothes for several years. Luckily we did not have to stand and have hems pinned up for them.

Right across the Delaware River from New Hope was Lambertville, New Jersey. The bridge over was a toll bridge—ten cents to cross. One felt one was really going somewhere when it cost a dime to get there. Lambertville boasted a liquor store, a Five & Dime, and the People's Store, an emporium of delights. It was there I saw a miniature violin, complete with carrying case and rosin for its bow, tagged at the lordly sum of one dollar and twenty-five cents. For me that represented more than two weeks allowance. I despaired that someone would buy the violin before I could save up the money and I checked weekly to see if the violin was still there. When I finally had the money in hand, the violin was gone! I was so disappointed the store manager, after checking the stockroom, told me he would put in a special order. Weeks passed and then finally the violin arrived. Inexplicably, instead of feeling joyful, I felt let down. I probably had expected to play it and make beautiful music instantly. And yet I can think of no other material possession I have yearned for as I did for that little toy violin.

Trenton, New Jersey was some forty minutes' drive down the River Road. We went there to buy shoes, always at the same store. There, first off, our feet were carefully measured and then, when the shoes were tried on, one stood in the Fluoroscope to check the fit. We put our feet in the machine several times, to see if there was sufficient wiggle room.

Every year or so we paid a visit to the Trenton Doll Hospital. There anything a doll of whatever sort needed could be taken care of—limbs restored, eyes made to open and close again, lost "mama" cries found, wardrobes replenished. Ria's and my particular dolls Hannah and Jane would need to have their canvas heads and faces repainted (with oil paints, I believe it was), like a makeover at Elizabeth Arden. When we picked them up after their stay in the Trenton Doll Hospital they looked as good as new but still just like themselves. One day in the time that lay ahead it may have been their unblinking yet expressive painted eyes that stopped Ria and me from trying out a bit of voodoo magic.

Trenton had a wonderful bookstore (the Travers Bookshop, now long gone) and, in a somewhat seedy part of town, a Russian steambath. The steambath regime always left me with a splitting headache but that would not deter me because we always ended the outing by eating the best (like the rice pudding, unequalled to this day) of all ham-and-cheese-on-a-roll sandwiches our mother got from a particular delicatessen.

The other memorable thing about Trenton was the fact that our route into the city took us right by the Toddle House, an eatery specializing in hamburgers where once our father had hung his sign—The Water Monkey—and specialized in American antiques. And our mother, in partnership with Tom Matthews's sister Peggy, set up a tea shop on the banks of the canal running just behind the house. Possibly this was done to lure customers to the antiques. In any case, once everything was ready for business, the two entrepreneurs hid behind a morning-gloried trellis and prayed that no customers would come. I'm not sure whether or not any did.

Trenton was my first home. I was nameless for most of the time there. My parents could not decide what to call me other than Baby. I don't believe a formal baptism was planned but a godfather had been chosen, A.R. Orage, an Englishman of literary distinction and a follower of Gurdjieff whose movement my parents were interested in at the time. Orage proclaimed that he would not be godfather to a nameless child and that he would take Baby off in her perambulator and bring her back with a proper name. One wonders how a walk on Trenton's sidewalks inspired him with the name Griselda. He left it to me to choose a middle name. At one point I chose three, one of them being Cenerentola, a name Bousie had suggested, fortunately not approved by my mother.

Orage was a wonderful godfather, his presence and his presents a pleasure. At Eastertime he gave me a large chocolate turtle whose shell lifted up to disclose a slew of miniature chocolate animals. And, just when I had discovered the ruse of reading under the covers, he provided me with a flashlight that had beams in red and green as well as white.

There were many visitors who came to the farm, some regularly, some only once or twice, and, in the case of Tom Matthews and his family, so frequently that they seemed even more like family than our various aunts, uncles, cousins, and grandparents. Tom and our father had been the closest of best friends ever since their Princeton college days. Tom and his wife, Julie, were the only adults we called by their first names from the very beginning. Tommy and Johnny, their two oldest boys—two more were to follow later—were our closest non-farm playmates. That is when they came to the farm or when we visited them at Boothden in Newport at their grandfather the bishop's place. When we very occasionally saw them in Princeton, it was a bit of a sticky wicket. This not only because the farm provided more for us to do but, in Princeton, the older they became the less comfortable they felt about having Maria and me—girls!—as playmates. They'd be in for some teasing from the boys who were their usual companions.

We often had picnicking days with Tom, Julie, Tommy, and Johnny. A favorite Jackson/Matthews picnic spot was Tinnacum, north of Lumberville. I don't know why the adults weren't nervous wrecks there. The picnic spot was on the edge of a cliff plummeting down to the lively Tinnacum creek. To get down to the water, there was a narrow, twisty path. It's a wonder that none of us fell off either the ledge or the path.

We also went over to the Jersey shore, to slightly commercialized Mantoloking or to the Phipps Estate where there was a stand of pine barrens and then a wild beach, nothing man-made in sight. We kids swore we could smell the sand and sea almost from the start of the trip. On the way home there was always a stop at a simple eatery where our parents had a glass of beer and ate oysters, and we had popsicles. But on one occasion our parents decided we should each try an oyster— to us a daunting prospect. We stood in a row. An oyster was popped into each unwilling mouth. "Now swallow." Urgh! Then Tommy put his finger down his throat. Up and out came his oyster. The rest of us followed suit. We stood in the row, a rejected oyster on the ground in front of each one. We thought it was hilarious. The grownups, it seemed, did not share our sense of humor.

Tom worked at *Time* magazine and would eventually become its editor-in-chief. He expected greater attainments from our father and I think it is safe to say that no one else in his life mattered more to him. When the friendship came sadly to a dead end, he never quite laid the matter to rest. My special bond with Tom was our shared devotion to my father. Tom's wife, Julie, in turn was my favorite mother figure beyond my own. We kids felt entirely comfortable with both of them. They were rather like a second set of parents and Tommy and Johnny were like brothers. We felt related to their relatives and do to this day.

We did not really, however, tie Princeton to the Matthewses. There were other people there we went to see more often, among them the Harts. Mr. Hart was another Princeton classmate. The four Hart children were all exceedingly bright and interesting. Saki, the youngest, was something of a child prodigy. I can see her now racing musically along at the piano, her little feet dangling way above the floor. David, the oldest, was particularly adventuresome. At one point he was into the drums. The whole house reverberated for hours on end. As an adult he became an authority on the tribes of the Riff Mountains, his anthropological bent having been stimulated by the Cherokees on our farm. He ate his pusher when he came to visit—but this I have to explain.

We kids each had our own silver pusher to help get peas and such onto our forks. Guests had to make do with little squares of bread meted out by Bousie. Every time he handed David one, though, David would immediately pop it in his mouth and eat it. Bousie would hand him another and another. David would down them all. We were goggle-eyed.

We associated Princeton with special treats—the fourth of July fireworks in the stadium, ice-skating shows—and with the dreaded dentist, Dr. Kaiser. As for the treats, there was one particular never-to-be-forgotten fireworks display finale. At the end of the football stadium two firecracker train locomotives came from opposite directions, collided, and transformed into a basket of flowers which, in turn, became the American flag amid a panoply of rockets' red glare.

As to Dr. Kaiser, the only pleasant thing about visits to him were the stacks of movie magazines and *True Confessions* we could browse through while waiting for the torture chamber. The principal information gleaned from this reading material seemed to be what various Hollywood stars wore or did not wear to bed.

What really made Princeton an important place in our childhood was the Harpers. George McClain Harper's field was literature. He was the author of numerous books, many of them concerned with poetry, the English Lake poets especially, and Wordsworth in particular. Mr. Harper was a distinguished professor at Princeton University, where he taught for many years. He considered my father the most brilliant student he had ever had even though Bousie often cut classes when he deemed himself busy with more pressing matters or already knowledgeable about the day's lecture. In addition to holding him in the highest regard academically as well as admiring his poetry, Mr. Harper loved Bousie like a son. This affection spilled over to include our whole family.

The Harpers were the only people I've known, I'm sure, who never did a poor or bad thing in their lives. They seemed to have an innocence come from some other era, yet they were entirely aware of the one in which they lived. They were both lively and formal. In public they never addressed each other by their first names. It would be, "Will you take some more tea, Mr. Harper?" (our visits were usually around teatime). "Well, Mrs. Harper, that would be very nice indeed."

Both of them had twinkles in their eyes; both gave off an air of an upright nature. One could not imagine misbehaving in their presence. When Mr. Harper uncovered the fact that Wordsworth had fathered (and abandoned) an out-of-wedlock child, he was very disturbed. Nonetheless, he did not hide the facts under the carpet.

In the room where we had tea, generally sitting in a circle and balancing our tea cups on our knees, there was a photograph hanging which I was very drawn to. It was of the poet Robert Southey's grandson. That portrait, overheard conversation, and pictures of the English Lake District gave me a keen desire to one day go to the lakes. Perhaps I would meet Southey's grandson.

Once Mr. Harper and I were standing on the front porch of his house. He'd just been showing me a robin's nest in one of the nearby bushes. Along the street—Mercer Street—came a man with disheveled white hair. Mr. Harper doffed his hat— he always wore one when outdoors—and bent over in a slight bow. "Good afternoon, Professor Einstein," he said. The white-haired gentleman bowed in return. "Good afternoon, Professor Harper," and off he trotted down Mercer Street. "That was a very famous scientist," Mr. Harper told me. I was deeply impressed.

The Harpers had a son and a daughter, both grown up and living away from Princeton. The daughter, Isabelle, and her husband were involved in a scientific experiment to discover how tame a wild animal might be if it was raised solely by humans, never knowing its natural parents or habitat. Their "guinea pig" was a lynx, which they had raised from birth, a beautiful and rather large creature. When Isabelle came to visit her parents, the lynx came too and was often not confined in its cage. The idea of Mr. and Mrs. Harper living with such a wild creature was quite amazing to entertain. But then, the Harpers, however Victorian genteel they might seem, were full of surprises.

Mr. Harper's death itself contained surprise. After lunch, his custom was to go for a nap and sit, his hat pulled down over his eyes, in a rocking chair on the back porch. On his way out the door, he would always pause and say, "I'll see you later, Mrs. Harper," though, maybe with no one else there he said

Belle. After years of this routine, one particular day he paused at the door and said, "Good-bye, Mrs. Harper." Mrs. Harper mulled these puzzling words over and after a bit went out to the back porch. There was Mr. Harper sitting in the rocking chair, his hat pulled down over his eyes as always. But he was dead.

Mrs. Harper had complete faith that she would eventually rejoin him. She had work to do, she told those concerned about her. All Mr. Harper's correspondence, his papers, his books to sort out. About a year later (this was in the late forties) Mrs. Harper became ill. The doctors summoned the Harper children to come immediately. Mrs. Harper was in a deep coma on her deathbed. As Isabelle and McClain waited by her bedside, suddenly Mrs. Harper sat bolt upright, opened her eyes, and proclaimed, "I am not going to die now. I still have a great deal of work to finish." The doctors could not explain it—they had never seen anything like it before.

Mrs. Harper returned to the house on Mercer Street, continued to serve tea, continued her sorting-out job. One small, but to me very meaningful, sorting-out she did was to send me a four-volume collection of English poetry that Mr. Harper had used and annotated in his student days. Each book was inscribed to me: "Griselda Jackson with love / Belle Wescott Harper." "Griselda Jackson / George McLean Harper / used these when / he was young, loved them / and felt he owed them much / He would want you to / have them for he loved / you dearly - B.W.H." "Griselda Jackson / who all her life has / been dear to / George McLean Harper / & / Belle Wescott Harper." The fourth volume's flyleaf has been lost, but pasted on the back inside cover is a 1925 newspaper clipping announcing the death of Southey's grandson. I finally knew his full name—Alan Lancelot Southey of the picture I used to dream over during tea at the Harper's.

When Mrs. Harper's work was finally done, she went to spend her last years with her daughter Isabelle and the lynx. She was waiting for the time when she could again be with Mr. Harper. When she was—and she must have been—I'm sure Mr. Harper greeted her, "Mrs. Harper, how happy I am that you are here."

If we kept on driving north on the main road through New Hope, we would come, after a few miles, to the turn off into the Cutalossa, one of the special places, home of our special familiars, the Daniel Garbers. Their place, which today still looks much as it did over a half century ago, seems almost like a composed painting, as perfectly balanced and choice as a painting of it would be. It lies in a narrow valley through which the lively Cutalossa stream flows—along a stretch of its path a verdant field kept cropped by a flock of sheep. There was a small mill building, its dam creating a little waterfall below which the stream widened into a fine swimming hole.

Across from this area the house, studio, and a cottage perched on a sloping hillside. The sheep occasionally grazed there to keep the weed growth down.

Mrs. Garber had a somewhat severe appearance. She was tall and wore her hair in a tight braid around her head. She gave the impression of being aloof but in fact she had a very warm heart and was anything but. My parents and I lived in the Garbers' cottage for some while before the move to the farm. Mrs. Garber did not think highly of the mode of child rearing popular at the time. It prescribed strict scheduling, the maintenance of an inflexible time-table for when the various baby tendings should occur. If a child was put in a playpen, that was that. No matter what the baby's complaints, no attention was to be paid until the appointed hour. Mrs. Garber told me that I often squawked loudly under these conditions and that, if the coast was clear, she would come over and play with me on the Q.T.

Mrs. Garber had a passionate side that she kept pretty much under wraps. But when there was a storm and the Delaware waters were roiled up and threatening flood, she would take off on foot for the river banks and race along them against the debris floating swiftly by.

Mrs. Garber had a lifelong passion for Joan of Arc about whom, as well as the history of Joan's time, she had read everything available in French as well as English. She composed her version of St. Joan's story and wrote it down in beautiful India ink calligraphy, each spread of pages illustrated with meticulous pen drawings. It was a true work of art but she never was quite satisfied. She would redo pages where some tiny detail displeased her and nothing would persuade her to "go public" with her small, exquisite masterpiece. The Garbers' two children, John and Tanis, were similarly talented.

Daniel Garber said that Mrs. Garber's opinions in regard to his painting were the most cogent that came his way and counted more than any others . The impression one had of him was quite different from that of his wife. He had a glint in his eye and much of the time a positively jolly air, qualities captured in a charcoal self-portrait that hung in a back hallway of their house (many of his finest works hung throughout their home). In it he is glancing over his shoulder, a roguish and delighted expression on his face. He looks like something of a handful.

Daniel Garber was very welcoming when we visited him in his studio, though as often as not he would be off with his little black Ford pickup painting somewhere in the countryside. But whether he was there in his studio or not, we would always drop in. In its anteroom was a press on which he printed his etchings, watched over by a life-size sawdust-stuffed dummy. It must have been used sometimes in lieu of a live model. The studio had a lovely aroma of oil paint, turpentine, ink, and wood and it was always full of paintings—a few on easels, and many others stacked up along the walls. There were tall windows for light and, at one end, a small balcony from which Mr. Garber could see his sheep down by the stream. One day he was doing just that when he was struck with a heart attack and plummeted over the railing to his death.

We often took our guests on a drive up, if not to call on the Garbers at least to see the Cutalossa. We just wanted to show them the place. To see it was to see a little Shangri-la.

Mr. Garber was not a modernist. He found the way he wished to show the world he loved and, quite amazingly, he managed to earn his living uninvolved with and unsupported by any art scene. His daughter Tanis told me he would be flabbergasted by the kind of prices his paintings garner nowadays, a few thousand being the most he ever sold his work for in his day.

Among our "other" places was Brookwood, our maternal grandmother's place at Cooperstown, one she had known since her own childhood. Avoiding Bucks County's muggy river-bottom weather, we went there every summer for a month. Sometimes we drove—a long haul on small roads, through small towns. To pass the time we had contests to see who counted up the most cows or horses from his or her side of the car. We sang "You Are My Sunshine," "Row, Row, Row Your Boat," "Ninety-nine Bottles of Beer" ("For goodness sakes, you kids, sing something else"), and we kept our eyes open for Burma- Shave signs (Does your Husband / Misbehave? / Grunt and Grumble? / Rant and Rave? / Shoot the Brute / some *Burma-Shave*.) We looked forward to arriving at the perfect-for-a-picnic place our father had discovered. If not by car, then we would go by train on the Phoebe Snow Line, boarded at Lambertville and traveling for a good stretch of the way along the Delaware to Binghamton where we'd be met. The train had Pullman accommodations. The conductor remembered us from year to year. He knew we liked to have pillows to snuggle on and tall glasses of freshly made lemonade, each sporting a maraschino cherry. Somewhere along the route, the train passed the conductor's home. He could wave to his family and we would too. In fact, waving from the train was a kind of game. Would the wavees wave back? Most of the time, they did. Years later, when our mother moved away from the farm to a tiny village—Raven Rock—on this same line, we could ask the conductor to ask the engineer to stop and let us off on the meadow right across from her house.

Either way we journeyed, by car or by train, it was a long haul but more than worth it. Brookwood was a dream place for a summer vacation, a big homey country house on a lovely piece of lake-front property. Because I was the oldest, I was privileged to have a particularly enchanting bedroom. It was at the head of the main staircase and had a little latticed inner window that looked out on the stairwell landing where the nightlight glowed and one could imagine one was looking out at a street in an Alpine village. My room had windows overlooking the driveway; out beyond it, lawn leading to the pine woods. At night sometimes—my grandmother told me to keep an ear cocked—one could hear the ghost of a long-dead gardener raking the gravel. Ria actually did hear him and so did others.

The kids slept in the nursery area. And they ate in the children's dining room while I, after attaining the lordly age of ten, ate the main meal of the day with the grownups. That was quite another dining experience. In the grownups' dining room not only were we waited on, but there were various courses, each served on different china and involving different cutlery. And there were fingerbowls with lemon verbena leaves floating in the sparkling crystal. My privileges did not, as far as I know, bother the kids. After all, I had had my stint in the nursery as well as the children's dining room. There, underneath the round table top, there was a boxed area formed by the table legs. This was very handy for hiding away bread crusts and other things one didn't want to finish eating.

At Brookwood we got to know not only our Grandma Katie and her second husband, the adorable "Uncle Neddy" Chapman, but some of our aunts, uncles, and cousins as well. Grandma Katie was a delightful grandmother. She enjoyed her grandchildren, whereas she hadn't paid all that much motherly attention to her own brood of seven. She left the daily motherly affairs to Fraulein, the much-loved German governess.

On frequent trips to Europe with a full contingent of children and servants, Grandma Katie would be off seeing the sights and socializing while Fraulein kept up a sort of home front. Grandma Katie took more interest in her children once they entered their teen years.

With her grandchildren, however, Grandma Katie was hands on. She liked us to tumble around on the big cushy living-room couch and on her as well. She would tell stories—especially ones about ghosts—recite poetry, sing songs, her big dark eyes wide with excitement. Sometimes she would play her violin, clearly out of practice but not of enthusiasm. She was keen on fortune telling, the Ouija board, and levitation. Several times she had us stationed around a card table trying to get in touch with some spirit or other. "Aaah, we're making contact." Her eyes were as big as saucers. "Grandma Katie, stop pushing the table. You're pushing the table, Grandma Katie."

Grandma Katie was the kind of person well described by the exclamation "What a character!" A genealogist found some trace of a gypsy and a Bourbon nobleman in her family tree. Perhaps the gypsy strain flavored her personality. Orphaned at birth, she was raised by her aunt—our great-great-aunt Marie Jermain. Every summer we were taken to visit this ancient lady at Hedgelawn, the Jermain family's place on the outskirts of Albany. Great-great-aunt Marie was quite formidable from our point of view. She was hard of hearing and used a tortoise-shell ear trumpet. If one talked too quietly, she said, "Speak up. Don't be a mumbler." Then one would speak louder and she would say, "Don't yell like that. Where are your manners?" This made conversation difficult.

But after tea, served in large cups on oversized saucers, we would be released. We liked to run up to the attic where there was an array of stuffed birds—some relative had been an amateur ornithologist.* Then we would explore the grounds. A large pillar-fronted mansion (still standing, without its grounds, on the old Albany–Troy road), behind it a building that long ago had served as a kitchen, and nearby what had once been slave quarters. Our great-great-grandfather J.B. Jermain had seen to it that the grounds ran down to the river's edge, that the railway station was built an easy half-mile carriage ride away, that the church he had built and the family attended was a similar distance away in the opposite direction, and that there was a special back entrance to the Albany Rural Cemetery, where the family burial plot was. He was a man of great wealth and prodigious philanthropy. Grandma Katie inherited a large fortune and—having no understanding of and, one must add, no common sense about finances—managed to go through it, probably not helped by the 1929 crash. Towards the end of her life she had to sell Hedgelawn and its contingent property, her Washington Square house, the place in Southern Pines, North Carolina, and, alas, Brookwood. But this was some time after our summertime days.

Brookwood sat on a two-mile point on Lake Oswego north of Cooperstown itself. Around the house the lawns stretched down to the lake edge or back to the pine woods that lined the driveway or over to the carriage house still full of sleighs used once in wintertimes and various carriages used in preautomobile days. And by it, the door to the garden. To open this door

* Our grandfather's grandfather had been one of Audubon's sponsors.

was like entering the secret garden itself. It had been designed by our grandfather, Frederick DePyster Townsend, who was a fine landscape architect. When one opened the door, the first thing one saw was a large rectangular flower-bordered greensward banked on one side with an ever-blooming profusion of flowers, above which was a fruit garden—gooseberries, raspberries, apples, grapes. On the opposite side, a stand of pine or cedar trees screened off the kitchen garden—what delicious fresh vegetables we enjoyed! Beyond the grassy stretch and down steps to a lower level, there was an area for sitting under an apple tree, in the middle of it a pool with Pan cavorting in its center; below this area, the lake itself; opposite it, the garden house.

The garden house's ground floor was a place where canoes, paddles, sun umbrellas, watering cans, and other paraphernalia were stored. The upper floor, with its balcony and high arched French windows that opened out onto it, was a splendid place to use as a stage. Many a performance was put on there. Inside was a single regally large room furnished with handsome heavy wooden chairs with deep-red velvet cushions. Quite suitable for Henry the Eighth as far as we were concerned. There were shelves of books, many leatherbound, but loads for us to pull down and read, and there was a lidded window seat tucked under a corner window that was full of wonderful old photographs. I wish now I had purloined some of them. The garden house was a perfect place to play on the rare rainy day.

I learned to swim at Brookwood. My father took the direct method of pushing me off the deep end of the dock. I was horrified but there was nothing to do but dog-paddle to the shore and then I felt triumphant. We swam and played in the water a lot. Getting blue lips and goose bumps was the gauge for having to *get out of the water now!* There was a sizable sunken boat near the dock which we felt rather spooky about. It was a recurrent dare to swim underwater and explore the wreck.

At Brookwood we weren't particularly enthusiastic about the children whom Grandma Katie sometimes arranged to visit. We'd muster shyly through visits with these "intruders" and usually felt relieved when they went home. One of these was a distant cousin, Folger Oudin by name—a frequent visitor until . . . . One afternoon we invited him to join our club. There's some doubt that this club actually existed. But first, if he wanted to become a member and learn all the club's secrets, he would have to go through an initiation. This involved several challenges ending with having to spend time locked up in the tennis house by the then-unused courts. Folger complied. We locked him in, went off, and forgot about him. It turned out that there was a hornets nest inside the cabin. The hornets got angry, as hornets are wont to do, and attacked Folger. When he was rescued, he was in a sorry state and we were deservedly in the doghouse.

Brookwood is still there, much the same now as it was in our time, though its garden is not in its former glory and profusion and the charming decorations it subtly sported—elves peeking out among bushes, oddments of sculpture, the Ali-Baba-and-his-forty-thieves terra-cotta vats gracing the steps down to the Pan fountain—are mostly gone. Now Brookwood is under the auspices of The Cook Foundation set up by the son of the man who purchased the property from our grandmother. The board of this foundation hopes to preserve the place in perpetuity. Certainly it is preserved in our memories.

Other people, other places—I have only touched on a particularly special few. There are many others kept in mind's eye and heart. And after the fateful 1939 summer new friends who knew nothing of it came into our lives. We children were unusually fortunate in being exposed to the widest spectrum of sorts and conditions: from the very simple and nearly poor to the elegant and greatly rich; from upstanding bourgeois to unconventional artist. This was one of the great and unusual privileges of my youth. To meet someone I was not comfortable with, and possibly did not like, who in turn did not like me, was something extremely rare. But it could happen and did: once to my peril.

NOT FORGETTING
TO MENTION S.E.X.

One aspect of the thirties, very different from the way things are now, was that children could remain largely innocent about sex, only slowly in their own good time developing an active curiosity about sexual matters. Growing up on a farm, we knew about, but did not dwell on, procreation. We saw the rooster in action, we certainly knew what the ram was busy at when he was turned out into the flock of sheep, we were aware of the result that, in due course, would follow our cow's visit to the Slacks' bull on the neighboring farm. I watched our cow Sally calve and during the lambing season saw the births of many lambs. In fact, one year Bousie gave me a lantern to light my way to the barn so I could watch and even sometimes help. It was a season of especially difficult deliveries, as Bousie had experimented with the idea of crossbreeding our Shetland ewes with a Merino ram. This turned out not to be a good idea. That year there were many traumatic births.

As to sex between people, in general we did not want to go beyond romance. When there was kissing on the movie screen we tended to cover our eyes and say "Yuk." Of course, as we got older our curiosity level grew. Aside from peeking down into the kitchen through the ceiling vent in hopes of seeing Lloyd Owl kiss the Georgia Peach, we discovered—snoops that we were—an all-about-sex book in one of Marie's bureau draw-ers. It was not very informative. The only thing I garnered from sneakily reading it was that a man should treat a woman as if she were a violin.

We certainly wanted to stay clear of A.B.'s kind of hints about a dark and seamy side to the subject. Unknown at the time, he tried to seduce little Kathie, first by luring her into the hayloft with a silver dollar and exposing himself, and later, having found her alone in her bedroom, when she fought him off with tooth and nail. Walter Allen, Pauline's brother, who had already been in some trouble, got sent off to reform school for raping Darleena on her way home from school. We heard of it but we did not want to know the details and Darleena cer-tainly did not want to talk about them.

Then came the show at the Strand Movie Theatre in Lambert-ville! Maria and I were dying to be taken to see it, a "special" extra for one Saturday matinee only. Extras were a feature of movie-going back then: the Flash Gordon serial, Robert Bench-ley, the Three Stooges, the Eyes and Ears of the World Newsreel, the cartoons—a whole array of shorts preceded the featured movie. Now we could see a Birds-&-Bees one as well, twenty-five cents admission raised to thirty-five cents for this special event. Our mother was cajoled and dropped us off.

The poster advertising this occasion gave assurance that a doctor and a registered nurse would be on hand in the the-atre. And indeed they were, although whether they possessed the certificates of their profession was doubtful. The doctor, stethoscope dangling over his white robe, appeared on stage and pointed out the nurse who, in addition to wearing stan-dard nurse's garb, carried an oversized flashlight. She was there pacing the aisles, the doctor told the sold-out crowd of kids, in case anyone fainted or felt sick at his or her stomach; she would administer smelling salts or escort the victim out. On this note of reassurance, the lights were dimmed and the film began.

What did we see? A diagram of the female reproductive tract, nothing whatever about the male organ, though the word "sperm" was mentioned while we were shown a drawing of a host of them swimming up the vaginal passage. Then we were shown an actual birth (the doctor reminding us about the nurse's presence). This seemed to be a messy affair with much dwelling on the umbilical cord, the afterbirth, and the cleaning-up of a far-from-pretty baby. After that, and by far the longest part of the program, we were lectured about not getting pregnant before marriage, the dangers of syphilis and the white-slave trade, and how to avoid contracting the one and being lured into the other. It was a relief when the show was over and *Popeye* came on. All that we gathered was that birth was bloody; that we should not drink from cups provided at public fountains; that if we saw someone whose nose seemed to be being eaten away, we should find our parents A.S.A.P.; and that we should be wary of exotic-looking strangers who might enslave us. So much for sex education in the thirties. It was mostly left aside until we got near our teens, when our interest in the subject grew and our bodies sent signals and curiosity led us on. And what was so bad about that?

WHAT'S GOING ON?
WHAT'S HAPPENING?

News. What was happening in the 1930s? One way and another we picked up on a good many things.

Little pitchers have big ears. For instance, in 1935 the Hauptmann trial was going on in Flemington, New Jersey, not far from our home. My little sister Kathie—all of three—didn't know about the court proceedings but she certainly knew about the Lindbergh kidnapping. For days she was terrified that, in the middle of the night, someone would put up a ladder, crawl through her bedroom window, and take her away. "Don't be stupid," we said. "We're not rich and famous. Nobody would want to kidnap you." To no avail. It was, I think, one of Bousie's not-so-funny jokes that scared Kathie out of her Lindbergh fear. Bousie hid under her bed and, after she was tucked in, began to push it up and down. Then, just as she leapt out, he grabbed her ankles. It is easy to imagine what a scare that gave her. She shrieked for Annetta. Afterwards, instead of worrying about someone coming up a ladder and climbing through her window, she concentrated on checking under her bed and in the closet.

There was the radio. This was a large piece of furniture at the far end of Bousie's study. It ran on a car-size battery and could receive stations around the world, albeit with varying degrees of static. I picked up a few bits and pieces of the news from it and remember hearing some of F.D.R.'s Fireside Chats, but my main interest in the radio was the Lone Ranger program. I was allowed to listen to two of the three weekly episodes. Given the scheduling this meant that I had to choose between missing out on the beginning, the middle, or, worst of all, the ending of each story.

The first news I recall really listening to was the BBC broadcast of Edward VIII's abdication speech. I was moved. What true romance to give up a throne for the woman he loved! When I saw a photograph of the star-crossed lovers, however, I felt quite disenchanted. He did not look princely to me nor she like a royal princess.

As to keeping up with the news through papers and magazines, my main interest lay in *Life* magazine's photographs and the weekly installment of the Annie Rooney comic strip in the *Doylestown Intelligencer*.

Happenstance. We were driving home from an excursion to the Jersey shore. "Look, look," someone said. We looked and saw a great fiery explosion in the sky. It was 1937, the dirigible *Hindenburg* had met with disaster and gone up in flames.

We grew up in the Depression era and, though that did not affect our fortunate family, we were aware that many people were having a hard time. It was a matter of taking in things seen and figuring out their implications.

An elderly couple lived on a small property along the road over Jericho Mountain. Our mother, with me in tow, would stop in to call on them occasionally. They'd have been too proud to accept monetary help, but I think she took them food, probably vegetables from our garden. I noticed how bare the kitchen looked, how the cake of soap by the sink was a mere sliver, how there were just a few scrawny hens pecking around the backyard, the weedy garden mostly planted with potatoes. These observations added up. I knew that this old man and his wife were very poor. I used to worry that they didn't have enough to eat or that they might freeze to death in the winter. Years later I asked my mother about them and she told me that the old man had died and then his wife had starved to death.

Hobos frequently stopped by our farm asking if there was any paying job or if they could spend the night in one of the barns or if we would give them a meal.

One man arrived on a blizzardy November night while we were eating supper. His knocking had a desperate ring to it. Bousie opened the door and told him to come in. He sat at a side table and soon was wolfing down a well-laden plate of food. One could tell that he was extremely hungry. This happened just when our family was set to go to New York for a stretch. Bousie invited the man to stay on while we were away. He could tend the furnace, keep the kitchen's coal stove going, shovel snow off the roofs and entryways. And he did, staying in our house until winter was over.

Another hobo Maria and I have not forgotten spent several days at the farm. There was some work for him. He slept in the barn. In the early morning he came up to the house, washed his face at the pump outside the kitchen, and sat on the kitchen stoop to eat his breakfast. He was a cheerful, garrulous man and he didn't mind our company while he ate. After a week or so he told us it was time for him to move on. When he had finished his breakfast, he spread out a large raggedy cloth and showed us its contents as he checked them over. Not much there—a piece of soap, a razor, a thin worn wallet, a photograph or two, a pencil, a pair of socks, a few coins—his bindlestiff. He was ready to set off. We followed him across our front lawn and watched him going down the road. As he got a ways along, he began to sing and dance, jumping up in the air and clicking his heels together. A picture of joy! Charlie Chaplin's tramp was never a match for it. Maria wrote a little piece about our hobo which I included in my *Jackson Quarterly*. The only difference in our recall was that I thought he sang on the road and she thought he whistled. Maybe he did both.

I remember the view from the Pulaski Skyway on the way to New York City. One looked out over the Jersey Meadows, then a great expanse. Strewn across them as far as the eye could see were hundreds of makeshift huts constructed out of old lumber, pieces of metal, cardboard. Homes for squatters with nowhere to go. It was a sign of the Great Depression.

We used to go now and then to Mendham, New Jersey to visit Bousie's sister, our Aunt Nannie. Mr. Talmadge, her husband, had lost a fortune in the 1929 stock market crash. They lived on a rather grand estate but the mansion was closed up and they had moved into the caretaker's place. We kids would find a way to get into the mansion. The furnishings had been removed or were covered up with drop cloths. One could imagine its former splendor, however, for it had a ballroom now empty except for the chandeliers. It was the kind of place that called for servants. Now Aunt Nannie had just one—a faithful retainer who filled all bills from chef to chauffeur. When my grandmother died, he drove Aunt Nannie over to see Bousie. Maria and I also remember seeing him standing at attention in uniform, holding the car door while Aunt Nannie, swathed in black, emerged. As she stood looking through her tears at us, she could not hold her water. A thin, audible stream formed a puddle at her feet. The chauffeur did not bat an eye. It was a tableau that remains in my mind as a picture of someone stricken with grief.

But, as to the particular visit to Mendham: we were all seated at the table. Mr. Talmadge was about to carve the roast. There had been some political discussion about the upcoming presidential election (1936). Then the upshot—Bousie declared that he was going to vote for Roosevelt. Mr. Talmadge turned purple in the face. He slammed down his napkin and the carving knife he had been about to use. In no uncertain terms, he told Bousie to leave the house. Immediately. One could see Aunt Nannie holding her tongue. Mr. Talmadge was too enraged to calm down. We left with empty stomachs. I already was enthusiastic about F.D.R. because of David Owl's talk on the subject. The aborted Sunday dinner turned me into a staunch Democrat.

As to the war that was brewing inexorably in the thirties, I formed a sense of it through cookies, love, and the piano.

Cookies: These were the special Christmas Speculatins, from Germany which Mr. Gareis sent me every year. Then—1937, he wrote to tell me the box would be small because not so many ships were sailing between America and Europe. In 1938, the box was smaller. In 1939, no Speculatins came. Mr. Gareis wrote to the effect that things, unfortunately, weren't very friendly between America and Germany. People didn't want American children eating German cookies.

Love: What I learned about the coming war through romance is an odd tale. Bousie's sister Edith had left her husband in Grosse Pointe, Michigan and taken up a peripatetic life with her three daughters, moving from one place to another, the successive hotel accommodations less and less luxurious. In 1939 they all ended up at the Hotel Amsterdam in New York. A German freighter had been impounded; its crew were put up in the Hotel Amsterdam while arrangements were being made as to where they would go next. The three cousins, none of whom spoke German, somehow struck up friendships with three of the crew, two of them ordinary seamen who did not speak much English, the third an officer who did. In very short order all three girls got engaged—perhaps they wanted to escape the life they had been leading. Aunt Edith was naturally extremely concerned and she sent the oldest daughter along with her fiancé, the officer, down to the farm to consult with Bousie.

I knew about this and was very curious. While they were in the living room having the talk with Bousie, I peeked in trying to overhear what was being said. All I could garner was that it was a stiff conversation. The officer knew English but was obviously unpracticed in using it. At one point he and my father played a game of chess or checkers—perhaps that was to break the ice. What struck me was the officer's mien and appearance. He had a stiff, rigid manner, no smiles. He was handsome, blonde, and on his cheek he had a curving scar, a dueling scar it was. In appearance he personified the Hitler youth. I have no idea what Nazism meant to him.

The three cousins defied objections and married. Two of the new husbands, the seamen, were sent off to a detention camp. Their wives moved nearby and somehow managed to muster through the war years. The officer had an easier time. I think he was enlisted in some sort of work connected with the war effort. Quite amazingly, two of the marriages lasted; the third finally dissolved.

Piano lessons: It was because of Mr. Algore that I had an early sense that something was going on, something that should be stopped. Mr. Algore was our piano teacher, a Jewish refugee from Austria or perhaps Hungary who had somehow landed in Bucks County. Perhaps he had not only been separated from his homeland, friends, and family but from a budding musical career as well. He didn't talk about himself when he gave lessons but one felt he was a saddened person. He seemed fated to have bad luck. He fell down the stairs in the house where he rented a room and was laid up for a stretch. Then his car broke down and he could not afford to replace it. He could no longer drive to his pupils' homes, they had to be driven for lessons given in his small room up the stairs. He lost pupils because of this and eventually he disappeared from the scene. I hope some good luck came his way.

When our country went to war, I felt it was because of things that related to "our" Mr. Algore and against those personified by the disagreeable-looking man with the little square mustache. Mr. Algore was my touchstone for World War II.

ODDS AND ENDS

The family ate breakfast and dinner together, Bousie at the head of the table dishing up our plates and often ceremoniously sharpening the carving knife. For my fifth birthday Mr. Harper had given me a Wedgwood plate with a hunting scene on it and an ivy border. He gave Tommy Matthews one as well. I don't know if Tommy used his but I certainly used mine. I ate all my meals off it. The plate survived through my childhood years and the many changes in kitchen personell—I still have it.

As a family together we had the nightly reading-aloud and, too, the Sunday walk. The Sunday walk didn't always happen but it was a fairly frequent occasion. Bousie would get the walking stick David had brought him from the reservation along with the beautiful baskets the Indians there used to weave. We would put on hats and coats if the weather was chilly and off we'd troop on familiar trails from which more often than not we would branch to find something new.

The most wonderful find was the strawberry field. On property next to ours we discovered a large clearing mostly bordered by scruffy woodland. One could tell it had once been cultivated but had long since gone to seed. Here, surprisingly, wild strawberries flourished. The berries were teeny in size, huge in flavor. Once we knew about the strawberry field it became a yearly event to go back to it and harvest the berries. Picking them meant having a feast with as many berries ending up in stomachs as in the containers we were supposed to be filling up for the jars of strawberry jam that never got made. But for the Sunday walk we might never have known about the field.

And but for Earl Horn's tin lizzie, with its commodious backseat, in which all four of us could fit, we might never have known about the ringing rocks. Mr. Horn was one of Annetta's suitors. While we squeezed in the backseat, she sat in the front, maintaining the most upright of postures and a good deal of elbow room between herself and Mr. Horn. Propriety was in order. We were strictly admonished never to say "I need to wee wee" in Mr. Horn's hearing. This meant that no sooner were we all in the car and on the road than I needed to "go" and all through the drive was miserable holding on until we made a stop at a roadside stand and got ice-cream cones, which we ate there so as not to drip ice cream on Mr. Horn's automobile.

Finally (and in those days any drive over five miles seemed like a sizable journey—"Are we almost there?") we would arrive at the ringing rocks. The place was odd to behold rather than inviting. It was a beachlike area near the Delaware River and looked as though a giant had been striding along strewing large rocks and small boulders on his way and making a jumble that left no easy pathways on which to walk through or around it.

Mr. Horn had brought along some hammers and pieces of pipe which he doled out to us and with which we all began hitting and banging on the rocks. As I remember it, this created a veritable tintinnabulation of bell-like sounds in various pitches. Our ears rang with them as they floated skyward where, perhaps, the giant was listening.

Another expedition with Annetta and Earl Horn was a trip to see the ice skating show in Princeton. We didn't have tickets, so on the drive over I worried that every car heading in the same direction was heading for the ice show too. Would there be any seats left for us? Luck was with us. We got into the show and were entranced. The highlight was Sonja Henie gliding and twirling to a Mozart piece, dressed in green gossamer sparkling with diamonds. We could hardly wait to dance on our pond. Ma lugged down a small victrola with a stack of records, mostly Viennese waltzes. "Now," she said, "if you want to dance on the ice, you must start with learning the figures. Here's how you do a figure eight." We figure-eighted away but just as often skipped the discipline and tried to replicate Sonja Henie's moves. In our hearts, if not in actuality, we were dancing on the ice.

We could count on the ice in winters back then. Except for January or February thaws ponds, the canal, and sometimes even the Delaware River were frozen over and you could plan on having an ice-skating party. The most memorable one was for my New Hope classmates. It was at night. Several cars were parked on the roadside by the pond, their headlights trained on it. There was a bonfire on the island. There we cooked hotdogs and toasted marshmallows. A.B. was put in charge of the music—keeping the victrola wound up and changing the records. Bousie brought along an impressively huge pot of hot chocolate. What a splendid time we all had, dancing in the night!

Just as we could generally count on there being ice on the pond, we could generally count on feeling well. When we were sick and had measles, mumps, chicken pox and grippe (a des-

Me and the kids

ignation that covered almost all other ailments) and if a dose of castor oil didn't do the trick, we were put to bed and Dr. Leiby would come and check up on us every day, plying the tools of his trade—thermometer, tongue depressor, stethoscope—swabbing our throats with nasty dark medicine, giving us some of the large pink cure-all pills he kept in his black doctor's bag, conferring with Ma. When we were put to bed we were sick enough to want to be there. But then came the day when we could tell we were over the illness, perhaps a bit wobbly but in fact well. That was the day when I fully appreciated the little luxuries provided when I had been sick. I wanted to continue to enjoy them and that meant I had to feign still not being well enough to get up just yet. The main proof of my continued sickliness was not to leave a clean plate or finish the midmorning snack or the afternoon tea even though I had a ravenous appetite and food again tasted delicious. I would try to eat as much as possible but leave enough artistically arranged on the plate so that it would appear as though my poor appetite proved I was still sickly. I doubt I fooled anyone.

On one occasion when I was sick for a stretch in bed I accidentally made some sparkling orange wine. I disliked orange juice because it was the chaser we were given to drink following a dose of castor oil. I poured my glass of fresh-squeezed juice into a crystal perfume bottle, pushed in its stopper, and hid it under a pile of laundry in the closet. Four or five days elapsed. Then as I was drifting off in an afternoon nap a large popping noise resounded from the closet. The orange juice had fermented; it had turned bubbly the way apple cider does. It was delicious. I tried to duplicate it later but the results were miserable.

Remembering the pop of the fermented orange juice conjures up another popping—popcorn. Every now and then we made popcorn over the fire in the Franklin stove. The popcorn maker was a long-handled, lidded wire basket that had to be kept in constant motion, taking a good long time before the popping began—at first slowly and at random, then gradually at a steady full tilt, the corn blossoming into snowy-white balls we would sprinkle with salt and the finishing touch of melted butter. Perhaps we children would all be in our pajamas. Perhaps Bousie or Ma would read one more chapter while we munched. For sure when the bowl of popcorn was emptied we trooped off to our beds for the good night's sleep that would ready us for whatever lay in tomorrow's store.

BOUSIE AND MA—
A FEW MORE WORDS

When Bousie attended Princeton (Class of 1922) he lived off campus in the home of his widowed sister Peggy, The B.M.P. (The Beautiful Mrs. Paton), as she was called by the Princeton students. Bousie too was something of a campus legend. What attributes did he lack? Handsome, charismatic, brilliant (a Phi Beta Kappa who skipped more classes than he attended) and, quite exotically, a poet and a free spirit. He is probably the only person ever elected as a member of the Ivy Club without having taken part in any aspect of the selection process. He was, his classmates felt sure, the member most likely to succeed.

Following graduation, Bousie went off to Oxford—as did his boon companion Tom Matthews—and began to make something of a reputation on the literary scene. The highlight was his meeting with W.B. Yeats. They hit it off like a house on fire. Indeed, Bousie hit it off with just about everyone he encountered, a quality that he never lost.

Despite all the lures of being at Oxford and in England, Bousie cut his stay there short and returned to the States. He was determined to get going for his idea of a poetry book club, the Open Road Press. He had lined up a board of judges— Robert Frost, Vachel Lindsay, Hervey Allen, Padraic Colum,

Edgar Lee Masters, and a printer, William E. Rudge of Mount
Vernon—who would produce the books. What remained was
finding the poetry, Bousie proceeding on the assumption
that the poets were there to be found all across America.* He
outfitted a Model T Ford and enlisted a traveling companion,
one Vladimir Perfilieff, a White Russian Cossack officer who
had turned up in Princeton in 1919. Vovo, as he was called,
was going to paint the landscapes while Bousie knocked on
doors to find the poetry. They crisscrossed the country and put
many miles on the Model T. The funds ran short, no unsung
poets were found, and the Open Road Press folded before it
had gotten going, leaving in its wake a handsome brochure,
the Model T, and a little painting by Vovo. But the trip had one
major result. Early along the way Bousie met my mother.

He met her in the Brookwood garden. The day before, as
he and Vovo were arriving in Cooperstown, they noticed the
Brookwood pine woods and turned into the driveway to ask
if they could camp in them for the night. Grandma Katie was
immediately charmed. Of course they could camp in the pine
woods and wouldn't they join the party planned that very evening! (I'm sure Grandma Katie had an idea about her own
poetry.) Ma was not there but early the next morning she was
heading through the garden toward the lake for a swim or a
turn in the canoe and this coincided with Bousie taking a stroll
among the flower beds. Spell romantic chemistry with capital
letters! Bousie proceeded on his Open Road Press mission but
some weeks later, he turned back from wherever they were—

---

* If he scoured the country now in the very early twenty-first century, he would
indeed find poets hither and thither writing respectable and often very good poetry.
This I know from what I've seen in my publishing job.

Ohio?— to propose. Our mother broke her engagement to another man and not many months later Bousie and Ma were married.

Though they came from similar privileged and wealthy backgrounds, Ma and Bousie were very different from each other. One could deduce this just from the tale of their honeymoon in wintry Vermont. Ma was interested in being outdoors skating and skiing; Bousie was interested in introducing her to the wonders of C.M. Doughty's *Arabia Deserta*, which he read aloud into the wee hours.

In her family Ma was the fifth of seven, but since the last two children came after a considerable gap, she grew up as a somewhat spoiled youngest, affectionately dubbed Little-Wait-for-Me, her refrain as she tagged along on family walks. Her education was spotty and as a young woman she didn't have much on her mind beyond the pursuit of a good time. Being married to Bousie opened up many a new vista. Ma was quite a down-to-earth person, not one for dreams and certainly not one for doldrums. If you are down, pick yourself up and get on with things. She was a splendidly good sport, doing her best to fit into a life-style very different from the one she had been raised to expect.

Bousie on the other hand was a dreamer, one whose projects, such as the Open Road Press, were basically good ideas but either the timing was wrong or they contained an inherent streak of impracticality. For instance, he was deeply into organic farming, long before the term, let alone the practice, was in general use. He latched on to the merits of soybeans and planted crops of them. But back in the thirties there was no American market for soybeans.

Ma in her late teens

Bousie, Princeton student c, 1920
with professor Harper

Or take the three hundred black walnut trees planted for their lumber in the far distant future. They made regular cultivation in the fields more difficult. The walnuts themselves were labor intensive, hardly a viable cash crop. Still some credit is due. A mature black walnut tree is worth a good thirty thousand dollars. The trees were still far from mature when the farm was sold.

I felt very connected with Bousie's antique business. Aside from growing up with various pieces from the collection, there were others—a wonderful Noah's ark was one—that have stayed in my mind. And Bousie used to take me along on trips to a Mr. Bryher, a woodworker par excellence who could repair and even replicate furniture and, on top of that, fix clocks. In 1933 Bousie threw in the towel on his antique venture and sold his entire collection at an auction at the Anderson Galleries in New York. What poor timing! Not only was the Depression in full swing, not only was the day a Jewish holiday, but most important there was very limited interest at the time in early American furniture and various other household items. It was a truly remarkable and first-rate collection, one that Sotheby's or Parke-Bernet would give their eyeteeth for today.

All the time Bousie was having these disappointments and putting in long days of hard work, he still wanted to write poetry, keep on with his deep interest in language and his special project connected with the long-forgotten epics of C.M. Doughty for which he planned to produce a glossary. And all the while too he struggled with bouts of depression, a malady little understood then and one that afflicted the Jackson family to a serious extent. All of this was hard on Bousie and certainly on Ma as well. But never did either of them let any of their problems impinge on the very happy, busy, interesting childhood we were having—one in which Ma was there for us, taken to some extent for granted, and in which Bousie was the adored sine qua non.

During their courtship or early on in their marriage, Bousie gave Ma a beautiful little copy of William Blake's *Songs of Innocence* which she kept in her bedside table all her life long. There in his lovely handwriting are these words:

> *for Kitty   Through the years   through ice*
> *and through fire my love and my life always*
> *Schuyler*

Things didn't work out like that in the long run. Yet the sweet passion in the words still reverberates, echoing in the halls of my childhood memory.

THE RUIN

The Jackson Quarterly News Section
July 1939

The editor is sad and lonesome without his little Yamie a pet lamb who was runover by a car.

The old ruin across the road which is on the jackson's Farm has been rebuilt to a lovely little stone house in which shall live Miss Laura Riding, Mr. Robert Graves, Mr. David Reeves, Mr. Alan Hodge and Mrs. Bearal Hodge. All famous writers from England.

Mrs. Jackson is in the hospital, sick in Philadelphia.

Haying has started and all the crops are growing wonderfully.

The Mathews boys have visited for a few days.

The cook for the house across the road is named Elythen Owl from Cherokee Indian Reservation.

The children including the Editor are sleeping in the playhouse, which is fun.

The Editor is collecting bird feathers and has a nice lot.

The Writers as well as Frank Baisden an artist are living in the Jacksons' House for the time being.

Ben Jackson is five and had a wonderful Birthday Party on Wednesday June 21th, tho his Birthday was on the 18th.

The Editor has a little bald headed chicken, whose name is called Chicky. Chicky was killed, sad to say. Latest News:

The Editor's Pigeons are multiplying rapidly.

The editor has a new wireless radio.

Miss Ridings sister is here also.

The children have a little puppy named Lucky.

The Ruin

This was something new and interesting! The Ruin was going to be rebuilt. We kids were not particularly curious at first about why—we were interested in watching the transformation of a weedy cellar and a jumble of stones into an actual house. After school we'd rush over to the site to see the work-in-progress. The workmen were usually finished for the day by then and we could snoop around and inspect things without getting in anyone's way. Sometimes the contractor would be there along with Bousie discussing details. Bousie was a stickler for details, especially as to how the cement between the stones should be pointed in the manner of the Owls' early-eighteenth-century house. Not many weeks went by before we were able to go inside the structure and see how the rooms were laid out. Finally large boxes from Sears Roebuck arrived—the fixtures for the kitchen and the bathrooms. Doors and windows were installed, the floors refinished. Everything was so shiny new, the house didn't seem quite real, but we thought it was a very nice house indeed.

Now we became curious to see the future occupants. We gathered that they were writers. We thought they must be important people. After all, a new house had been built just for them. They had sailed across the ocean and were staying in Princeton but they would be moving in soon. One late May day—it was a nice sunny one—we were put on alert. The people were coming for tea and a first look at the house. We should tidy up a bit and be around so that they could meet us.

They arrived in two cars. One went directly over to the new place; the other turned into our driveway. Lined up by age, we stood in a row and shook hands. This is Miss Riding and this is Mr. Graves. The tea party assembled on the lawn near the railway-station roses. We sat quietly on the periphery and observed—all eyes.

I thought Miss Riding a curious sight. She was wearing clothes that seemed to me more like a costume than everyday wear. Maria remembers a sort of elaborate hunting jacket, bright red. She was wearing dangling jewelry and I think she was carrying a parasol or a fan. She noticeably had on makeup; one could see the layer of powder on her face. Her looks were intriguing. One didn't usually see ordinary people wearing ankle-length skirts or putting on makeup in the daytime back then. One minute she would seem almost ugly; another, she would look like a regal personage, maybe Egyptian, from long ago. She had very blue deep-set eyes and brown, bushy, wiry hair held back with a headband or a ribbon. Her voice seemed rather odd. She had a bit of a nasal twang and behind her English accent lurked a more plebeian American-city one.

Mr. Graves was large and burly and looked as if he had bad breath, as indeed he did. His attention seemed almost entirely focused on Miss Riding. Was she comfortable? Would she like a pillow to sit on? Did she want more milk in her tea? Was it too sunny, too breezy? Crumbs from the tea biscuits kept getting caught on her lip or in the corner of her mouth. Mr. Graves would alert her about them and often dab them away with his napkin. It seemed that Miss Riding's face was numb on one side so she couldn't tell when she needed to wipe her mouth. This condition made her smile just a little bit askew.* I did not feel drawn to either of them. I felt somehow disappointed, a

---

* Later I learned that this numbness was a result of Laura's having leapt from a third-floor window in London because one Geoffrey Phibbs, an Irish poet, did not reciprocate her ardor for him.

feeling that was not much improved when we were introduced to the others—David Reeves, Beryl and Alan Hodge. Reeves only stayed on the farm for a short while so I have no recollection of him beyond his name. Beryl—a grownup in our eyes, but probably hardly out of her teens—left little impression beyond the overriding one we soon took note of which, Maria and I agreed, was that she had a big crush on Robert Graves. "She's all googoo eyes," we concluded. For some reason I liked Alan Hodge the best of the lot. Perhaps the least affected, he seemed the most familiar. Miss Riding, whom we were soon invited to call Laura, seemed to me to be more like an actress than a regular, everyday person. Mr. Graves, whom we were soon to call Robert, seemed rather like a subservient butler. He did not look as though he was feeling either happy or well. Altogether, yes, I was disappointed. They were not how I imagined "famous writers, poets" would be.

Although it gave just the merest hint, that sunny May afternoon was the beginning of a rent that would soon appear in the fabric of our life on the farm. Our closely knit camp—all of us, children and adults, together as one unit—was faced with another one, that of these visitors—who were going to be around, as far as one could tell, "forever," sharing regular daily life with us. We children could not readily flow into a new family unit in such short order, try though the grownups did to include us, to draw us in. Bousie and Ma (who had been seeing them for some weeks before they came to the farm) had, on the other hand, fast become part of the new grouping. It was perfectly plain to see that Laura was the leader and it was perfectly plain to her, if to no others, that I had some problems with that.

I did not like the way the other grownups treated her. "Yes, Laura." "Of course, Laura." "You're right, Laura." I did not like Laura's acceptance of their deference. I wasn't comfortable in the heavy atmosphere—all the hustle and bustle, all the talk. Once, when crossing the front lawn, I passed them all sitting in a circle, no one speaking. Then Robert said something and Laura snapped at him, "Be quiet." And he was. I did not like the way either of them had behaved—he subservient, she dictatorial.

Now when I said "we" or "us" I meant Maria, Kathie, Ben, and myself. Bousie and Ma were so connected with Laura I could not tell either of them what was on my mind. And there were things that weighed on it. To start with, Laura's move from The Rise* into The Big House's guest room. This she did only a few days after coming to stay on the farm. Didn't she have the best bedroom in the new house? The one with a fireplace, built-in drawers, and a pretty view of the pond? Why should she come to live in our house when the new one had been especially built for her and her companions?

Very soon after Laura moved into our house, she and I had an open confrontation. Late one afternoon, Ria and I were sitting in Bousie's study and chatting with Tommy and Johnny. They were telling us about being in Mallorca where they had met Laura. And, guess what, she had put them in a story and the story was printed in a book. Tommy, eyeing the bookshelves, saw the book itself. Naturally we wanted to find the story, to see their names in print. So there we sat in a little huddle leafing through The Progress of Stories. And just when —"Here it is!," the opening line "Tommy and Johnny were two very good

---

* At first grandly named Nimrod's Rise, the new house came to be called simply The Rise.

little boys."—we had found it, Laura came bursting in on us. She was in a fury. She wrested the book out of Tommy's hands —"Don't take things from your father's shelves"—and turned to leave. I spoke up. "Our father always lets us take books from the shelves." Laura did not reply. She shut the study door with a bang and then we heard the click clack of her footsteps going rapidly up the stairs. We were stunned. How did she know that we were looking at the book and why did she mind our doing so? Had she been eavesdropping? I snuck into her room several times during the next few days when the coast was clear. I did not find the book. I looked in the bookshelves where Tommy had found it. It was not there although there were several other books by Laura Riding including a new collection of poems in which a copy of Bousie's *Time* magazine review was tucked. The poetry was way over my head. I gave up the search for the story book.

The presents—the jewelry—did not improve things as far as I was concerned.

Laura had a large jewelry box, a handsome polished wooden one. We had never seen anything like its cornucopia of gems—crown jewels they seemed to us. There weren't any highly valuable pieces but it was an interesting, tasteful, mostly old-fashioned collection. Laura was very relaxed about letting us rifle around in the jewelry box and she was very generous as a bestower of gifts from it. I don't think Kathie garnered much, if anything, but Ria and I did. My inventory: a garnet necklace, an amethyst one, a pin with emeralds and pearls, another with pearls and a lovely topaz, a vividly green jade bracelet, a natural pearl pendant on a golden chain. Among other things, Maria was given an enameled clock locket and a gold ring with three stones from an Egyptian tomb

Laura had treasures in her trunk as well. From it I reaped a little antique beaded purse, a delicately carved ivory fan as well as a plain one, a silver box with a tortoise shell lid, some ancient coins, a few fancy buttons, some lace collars, and the pièce de résistance, presented to me by Robert—a sort of headband tiara of seed pearls embroidered on exquisite blue velvet. We'd never had jewelry though I knew the three-strand pearl necklace Ma wore was from my Grandma Budgess, my paternal grandmother, for me when I turned eighteen. So for Ria and me these jewels were an amazing treasure trove.

However, there was a hitch. I did not feel right about accepting these gifts since I harbored ill feelings about Laura. Well, out with it—I didn't particularly like her and surely she knew it. Why was she being so generous? I squirreled the treasures away in the little Pennsylvania Dutch hope chest I kept special things in but somehow I felt I was being bribed. If Laura intended to win me over with these gifts, she did not succeed. Soon there was another run-in, this time connected with the matter of breakfast in bed.

Ma had always kept up a small luxury of having breakfast in bed. She had a special tray with legs and a set of pretty dishes, including a little pot for coffee with a matching one for the scalded milk. We'd keep her company sometimes and stick around until she got up and did her morning exercises. One of them was standing on her head, something we not very successfully tried to do too. Breakfast in bed was a special Ma thing.

One morning as I passed the guest room, Laura called out to me and asked me to tell Pauline it was time to bring up her, Laura's, breakfast on a tray. I clumped down the stairs and through the living room, and stopped at the step down into the dining room. "Pauline," I called out loudly, my annoyance in my voice, "Laura wants her breakfast now." As fast as a flash of lightning there was Laura. Really the speed of it could not be explained. Anger was on her face, her hand raised—I could not say whether she had actually struck me or simply threatened to. "Don't you ever call me Laura to the servants," she hissed. And was gone. I was incensed. We didn't call Pauline a servant. She, like the others, was a helper.

And speaking of calling, why, I wondered, did Laura so emphatically call Ma Katharine when everyone else called her Kit or Kitty and always had? There was an unpleasant ring to the way Laura said Ma's name.

The new people arrived on the farm in late May or early June. Soon after that we children were let out of school. The great expanse of summer lay ahead and we could go barefoot! As always, we found plenty to do. We had always occupied ourselves without adult supervision, so we hardly needed Robert to be appointed—by Laura of course—to do just that, supervise and advise. He thought putting on a play would be just the ticket and duly wrote a one-act play about horses for us to work on, but we had too many other things to do and didn't have so much as one reading.

We were aware of the grownups being very busy too. One thing we knew they were busy at was "The Dictionary." It was going to be a ground-breaking work defining words in a new and precise way that would give the one exact, true meaning. While it was in the making—and one could understand that would take a very long time—this dictionary existed in a few boxes filled with index cards and slips of paper. Work on it involved talk more than anything else. Indeed, talk seemed to be the principal business of the grownups. I did not know what they were talking about, but I took note of the frequent meetings, indoors and out, some voluble, some in the main silent. I took note of the general atmosphere. It was ominous. It felt the way the long-ago tornado looked. The kids felt it too, I'm sure. Fraught is the word that comes to mind. Fraught with what?—that was the puzzlement.

Laura was the principle part of the answer to this question. She made things tense and intense. The word "relaxation" was not in her vocabulary, let alone "fun." To this day Maria remembers Laura's bedtime storytelling as something to be borne and wish quickly over.

Another part of the answer was our Bousie who simply wasn't "there" for us that summer. I didn't have a clue that the intellectual communion between him and Laura was fast becoming a romantic and sexual affair before our very (unseeing) eyes. What inner turmoil he must have been going through, given the moral precepts he held!

And then there were strange happenings, quite impossible to explain. The snakes at The Rise, for instance. When it had been a ruin we knew not to go down into the cellar. There were snakes in it, perhaps copperheads. Then when The Ruin became a new house, of course the snakes had moved to some other place. But one day as Robert walked down the stairs an infant copperhead fell from the crawl space above the stairwell onto the back of his neck. It gives one the shivers to think about it but the puzzler is how in the world could the snake have been there?

Yes, the atmosphere was fraught.

A good many people came to visit, to meet Laura, to discuss the work she and her circle were up to. Some of them spent time talking to us. I especially remember Robert Cantwell, a *Time* magazine writer. I showed him my Crayola drawing of "my troops"— I called it "All of Us." He seemed to know I had a special feeling about this drawing. He took it back to New York and had it framed and sent back down to me. And there was Elliott Carter. He must have asked me to play the piano. We must have hit it off for, not long after his visit, I received a homemade booklet of short piano pieces by him with titles like "The White House" and "Griselda Comes Home from School." And I remember Robert Fitzgerald and his then wife Eleanor looking to see what books I had in my bookshelf and suggesting how I might organize them better.[*]

The outside visitors brought a sense of excitement but even without them the atmosphere we were living in was highly charged. I didn't have a clue as to what it signified, but there was a great bustle relating to an earthquake in South America: it seemed that it had something to do with the work. It seemed that it had been willed to happen. And towards the end of the month, June, there was another flurry when little pitcher-ears perked up again: something about a blighted field, something about Ma having something to do with it. I may have heard the word "witch." I remember looking at the field that there was something peculiar about it. This was disturbing and mysterious to me because I had been noticing now and then that something was peculiar about Ma.

---

[*] Henry Chapin, our family friend from the other side of Jericho Mountain, told me years later that he had come over and been told that he didn't pass muster and should not come again. I don't think now that the recruiting efforts were going all that well. Many came but few returned.

In the mornings when I dropped by her bedroom to say hello she seemed odd somehow. She didn't seem to be quite connected when one talked to her and her conversation was scattered. And I noticed as she dressed, she often wasn't wearing any underpants—for some reason this bothered me. It seemed odd. Then one day she spent a strangely long time in the linen closet. She opened up an old trunk there, one filled with linens that were too elaborate for our use, and she began rearranging the neat piles of towels, tablecloths, sheets, making a jumble of them. And all the while she kept making strange humming sounds. When I asked her what she was doing, her answer— "Because I want to"—had an angry edge. I went off to play outdoors feeling very apprehensive.

At this point, the visitors had been living on the farm for about a month. We were getting used to it, though without enthusiasm. The group was too busy, too intense, too humorless, too Laura-this-Laura-that. We were on the outside and not anxious to be in. And we were not wanted in. As when the four of us were together in the front hall and Laura said, "We [we being her, Bousie, and Ma] are going to have a discussion and you children will be informed later." Then she shut the study door. Something was not right. We were not used to doors being shut on us.

Then came the night when the lid flew off what had been brewing, what I, and maybe my siblings too, had sensed. Something was not right.

Everyone was seated at our dining room table—the visitors, Bousie and Ma, Laura, and us. It was not usual for The Rise occupants to be eating with us and it was the first time Laura had taken the seat at the head of the table, Ma placed as if she were a visitor rather than the lady of the house. The meal was almost over. It had not been a pleasant one. Suddenly Ma stood up and announced,

"I am taking the children for a walk."

"Robert will go with you," Laura said.

"No he will not," Ma replied.

"Not now, Katharine," Laura commanded.

"They are my children," Ma replied, "and if I want to take them on a walk, I will do so."

Did Laura say "You will not"? It was at the very least implied. Ma pushed back her chair, got up, and turned toward the door. I had a feeling that I had to stand up to Laura. I stood up, my troops stood too, and we followed Ma.

Across the lawn we went and started on the boggy path heading to The Rise. Along came Robert. "Go away," Ma said furiously. He left. Next came Beryl and she was similarly rebuffed. Then came Alan Hodge. "Go back," Ma said. "I am taking my children for a walk." Alan turned back. (Why wasn't Bousie the first one to come? I wonder now.)

We proceeded. When we got to The Rise Ma said, "Let's race our boats in the stream." There was a little one where the ground sloped off into the woodlands at the back of the house. So there we were together at the stream's edge. We found our twig boats and counted: Ready, Set, Go! Ma made strange humming sounds. She was squatting by the stream's edge and I noticed again that she was not wearing her underpants and she was cheating at the game, dropping her twig boat in ahead of the count. There was something about a peach pit I can't remember in detail except that it felt ugly and the game ended abruptly. We clamored up the bank, Ma in the lead. There on the driveway area she stood facing us, her puzzled, worried children.

"What's the matter with you? Something is wrong with you," I said, my heart in my throat.

"Nothing is wrong with me," she replied.

"Yes, something is wrong," I persevered.

"No, I am fine," she answered.

"No, something is wrong with you," I said for the third time.

"No," Ma snapped and moved toward me. "Nothing is the matter with me. You are sick, Griselda."

She put her hands on my shoulders and drew me near and then her hands were tight around my throat and she was shaking me. Then I was on the ground, she on top of me, her hands pressing my throat. "I am fine," she said. "I am fine." I could not answer.

Then—there was Bousie! He threw her off me. He pulled me to my feet and saw that I was choking but not physically hurt. "You kids go home and go to your rooms," he told us. Then without a further word to us, he and Ma took a path leading into the woods. Much later, from my bedroom window I saw them on the high hill above the pond.

And home we went. As far as I recall, the grownups left us alone. No words of comfort or reassurance. Maria and I moved our beds up against the wall between our rooms. Little Ben, what went through his mind? Little Kathie, who did she have to talk to? They were only just five and going on seven years old. Ria and I babbled on. What had happened was someone's fault, that's what we felt and thought. And it wasn't Ma's, terrified and horrified as she had made us. It was Laura's. That was the answer that we came up with.

Over the next days we took to sleeping in the barnyard playhouse. It felt safer than being in our separate bedrooms.

When we got up the next morning Ma was gone. "She's in the hospital," we were told. Laura said, "She has pneumonia." We knew that to be a lie.

But she wasn't away for long. In less than a week's time we were told she was coming home, news we took in with conflicting feelings of relief and apprehension. Robert was put in charge of us. We were to help get ready for Ma's return by clearing the lawn of every twig, leaf, acorn shell. Meanwhile the grownups were busy in the house.*

When Ma arrived she looked foggy and sad. It was a very stilted meeting. Roused from sleep that same night, I looked out my window and saw an ambulance and my mother being taken away in a straitjacket. A few days later we were driven to the Philadelphia Hospital to see her. "Do you want to see your mother?" the doctor asked. "No." He told me our mother was sick and it was like falling down and getting hurt when skiing. This was no help. No, I did not want to see her.

Who could we confide in? No one but each other. It was all too strange to speak to others about and I did not do so for a good many years to come. I think now that I must have burdened my sister Maria with my talk. She would only turn nine in August.

Ma had made a brave attempt to come back but something

---

* They were, I learned some years later, busy, under Laura's instructions, sorting out Ma's things and throwing away whatever might be connected with her so-called black magic. Two items I never saw again were probably tossed out then. One was Bousie's mother's fox neck piece—one Ma never wore but which we played with liking its bushy tail and beady black eyes. The other was the painting in the organ room for which I had a particular fondness.

was still too wrong. She had tricked the doctors into thinking she was well when, in fact, she was far from it. Figuratively speaking Laura was still at the head of the table and Ma was still under her spell.

Laura was indeed at the head of the table several days following Ma's return to the hospital. And this was when I almost went under.

I was in my room, heard the dinner bell ringing, and started down the stairs. Halfway between the third and second floors I was stopped in my tracks by a great wave of fear. I was dizzy, there was a buzzing in my ears, I could hardly breathe, I was losing my self, I was going off my rocker. I clung to the banister and mustered all the self-command and courage I could. "Just hang on through supper and you'll be all right when you get back to your room," I told myself. "Don't let anyone see how you're feeling." During supper I said hardly a word. I could not clean my plate. I asked to be excused and willed myself to seem normal as I left the dining room, my legs almost visibly trembling, my head swimming, from somewhere deep inside a voice telling me, "Just get back to your room. You will be all right."

I got to my room, sat on my bed. I kept taking deep breaths to hold my panic at bay.

Then I heard the click-clack—Laura's footsteps were always resounding. I knew without a trace of doubt that she was coming and she was coming quickly and I, having moved my bed catty-corner to the door, was trapped. There was no place to hide, no exit. I was cornered and she was coming and I knew she knew the condition I was in. She was going to push me over an edge—that's what I believed and still do. That's what I knew. What could I do? I prayed. Her footsteps accelerated and she was at the door and she was full steam heading in a beeline towards me.

And then something amazing happened. As Laura came rapidly towards me cowering in the corner on my bed, it was exactly as though she came full force up against a glass wall. Bam! She keeled over straight backwards from the impact and lay prostrate, the sound of her fall reverberating. There was a rush up the stairs. 'What's happening?" "Laura has fainted!" I sat in my corner and felt rescued and safe. If one really needed God, He would be there: David Owl had told me that.

After this encounter, for me a very close call, there was a truce of sorts. There were still times when I stood my ground. Maria remembers one particular time when she was sitting on my bed and watching an argument, Laura furious, me adamant. It ended by the route Laura took quite frequently when things weren't going her way. She fainted.

Having failed to get me out of the picture, Laura took another approach. Robert Graves was returning to England (the Hodges had already gone) and wouldn't it be a great treat for me to go along? I was quite taken with the idea; my mind's eye filled with the Lake District, Southey's grandson, and the royal family. But it was becoming chancy on the high seas and beyond that, Robert probably pointed out the fact that he and I were not best buddies and what was he to do with me once we landed over there?* I had written my gentlemen correspondents about the trip and to a man they were relieved to hear it had been called off.

---

* Robert Graves did depart in late July or early August. He put himself in my bad graces by asking for the return of the velvet and pearl "tiara." Poor Robert—he had a nervous breakdown when he got back to England.

Instead, it was off to Cooperstown where I spent one unsuspecting night in my special Brookwood bedroom and the next morning found myself being driven to the other side of the lake where I was summarily deposited in a summer camp for girls. It is not hard to imagine how alien an experience it was. The camp term was two-thirds over, I was a stranger to the girls and counselors, and my mind was full of the recent events and worry about my sisters and brother. I could look across and down the lake and see the Brookwood lawn. I was miserable. This was not helped by the constant arrival of letters from Laura. She wrote about the kids and the doings on the farm, and assured me that she was taking good care of my pigeons. And always she wrote about how she loved me and I loved her whether I knew it or not or, if I didn't, I would, or should. These letters made me queasy. I barely read them before tearing them up into little pieces. I certainly didn't want my cabinmates to see them. I am not sure whether I answered any. What I gleaned, though, was that when I got out of my imprisonment—for so camp seemed to me—I should lie low and avoid any trouble with Laura. I felt I needed to do this so that I could watch out for the kids.

When I was let out and brought home towards the end of August, I felt estranged and wary. The kids, outwardly, seemed to have adjusted. Of course they hadn't. But that was our, the children's, secret. I knew I couldn't organize a let's-pretend-for-real running away.

I knew Laura had become something permanent. Bousie told me so in a roundabout way. This was by telling me that Ma was wicked and evil and that if I loved her, I couldn't love him. "Can't I love you both?" I asked. The answer was No, I had to

choose between them and by choosing him I was also choosing Laura, who was good, with the same degree of affection.
Later I saw that this approach about good and evil was Bousie's
way of justifying what he was doing, explaining what had happened to Ma. If she was evil, then he was doing the right thing.
It was a bitter pill he presented me with and I could not swallow it. One afternoon during this time, as I was coming down
the stairs to the main hallway, I saw and heard Tom and Bousie
confronting each other over just this same unacceptable good/
evil choice. That was their last face-to-face encounter.

Ma remained away and we put up with Laura's attempts to
be motherly. It was a boon when school started and we kept
busy keeping out from under foot. Then, thank heaven, Dorothy Simmons arrived. She came to the farm in early fall accom-
panied by her husband, Montague. He did not stay long as he
felt dutybound to get back to England and help with the war
effort. The Simmonses were devotees of Laura but somehow
they retained more independence than others we'd seen. Dorothy proved to be a wonderful buffer between us, the kids, and
the situation we had been in and were in still. She was a sculp-
tress and made the organ room her studio. We liked Dorothy
greatly and she, just by being herself and genuinely liking us,
gave us a sort of shield, something we needed very much. She
went a long way that fall and winter towards helping us get on
with everyday life.*

It was hard to be estranged from the person one had held
above all others and with whom one had always been one-

---

* Years later Dorothy and Montague told me that she had not wanted to have any
children but she had enjoyed us so much she changed her mind and had two of her
own.

self—no acting, no mendacity. That was no longer possible between Bousie and me. All through the summer of 1939 there were things I felt, things I thought, things that happened that I could not speak to Bousie about. And when I sent out signals, he did not see them.

A poem I wrote about my teddy bear that fall had buried within its dozen or so quatrains just such a signal. I was saying something very personal. This particular bit went as follows:

> Wherever I go he tags along
> And sleeps at my side each night
> Cause though times are hard when I sleep with him
> I always feel safe at night.

I handed it in to my English teacher who gave the poem an A+. Then I showed it to Bousie. He told me the poem was very good but he thought, especially since I was going to send it to some people at Christmas time, I should change something. Perhaps I could substitute a different wording so that it would read:

> Because as long as I sleep with him
> I always feel safe at night.

I felt very disappointed in my father. I didn't know the term then, but it smacked of mind control. My sister Maria calls it more aptly heart control. There had been many signs of that in the preceding six months. I duly obeyed, but, as far I was concerned, my poem had been ruined.

Fall and winter passed and Ma came home to the farm in the spring of 1940. I kept a cudgel under my bed and once actually threatened to use it. Ma's youngest brother, Uncle Jimmy Townsend, came with her and was as helpful as Dorothy Simmons had been. He was quite a gem and he had a very good sense of humor. For instance, when the cook—perhaps Waggee Katolster—served horse corn instead of sweet, Uncle Jimmy, after taking a bite, neighed. On Saturday afternoons we were subjected to the opera played at the radio's highest volume. Bit by bit we regained our confidence in Ma. Bit by bit our daily life felt more like it had before the visitors came. Ma, by the way, never criticized or spoke badly of Laura. I found this odd indeed.

Bousie and Laura meanwhile found an apartment in New York City and listed themselves as Mr. and Mrs. Jackson on the mailbox—so Uncle Jimmy (who would later refer to Laura as the "little witchy") informed us. Laura changed her wardrobe. Gone the long, flouncy skirts, the shawls, parasols, lace collars.

Bousie was miserably homesick for us and we for him. There were many letters back and forth. We wrote "Dear Bousie and Laura" because we had to. On occasional visits up to New York we brought our homemade presents for them both because we had to: Bousie had made that perfectly clear. We were mendacious: including Laura seemed the only way to hang on to our beloved father. But it meant we felt more and more discomfited.

When fall rolled around, our mother invited Bousie and Laura to return to the farm and live in The Rise. But this was awkward. There were times, especially on school days, when we didn't feel like going over to see them as expected. Sometimes I invented especially heavy homework and once was caught in the lie when Bousie found me playing tag in the big barn. As time went on we children gradually just wanted to be free of the pressure and tensions that Bousie and Laura's presence exacerbated. So it was something of a relief when in the spring of 1941—following divorce proceedings, of which we knew nothing—they packed up their things and moved to Florida. I think Bousie thought we would be so miserable without him that we would run away for real. He had not understood that some things had been ruined and never would be rebuilt.

AFTER WORDS

Afterwards. It was a long time before Maria, Kathie, Ben, and I talked to others about the events that followed Laura's appearance in our lives. Most of the people who knew our family had only the dimmest idea of what had happened, if even as much as that, and they certainly didn't raise the subject with us. And as for the new people who came into our lives after Bousie and Laura went to Florida, they had no notion whatsoever. In later years the subject came up with the few people who had first-hand knowledge and experience and, like us, were trying to figure it all out, a task that is to some extent impossible. Nothing I learned afterwards altered my twelve-year-old's view of the summer of 1939, when there was a touch of evil in the air and Laura was its source.

It was Tom Matthews' idea that Bousie and Laura should meet. It would be, he thought, two brilliant minds together. Something good might come of it. One wonders why he wasn't given pause by certain experiences he had had when staying with his family near Laura's headquarters in Mallorca. For one thing, Laura had suggested to him that it would suit everyone if Tom's wife, Julie, would bed down with Robert Graves since she, Laura, was no longer doing so. Tom did not take up this suggestion. Then he faced a separate dilemma. Laura was working with him in connection with a novel he was writing.

They met for daily sessions. Then one day when Tom arrived at the appointed hour, Laura was not there. Instead there was a note. In it Laura said that she knew Tom was struggling with his passion for her. If he couldn't put it out of his mind during the lessons, he should leave the study instantly; there would be no more lessons. On the other hand, if he could put his feelings aside, he should wait for her; lessons would proceed. In either case, nothing would be said. Tom remained but he did not dare to say that he was not struggling with any such passion for her; he just wanted her valuable advice about his writing. Seeing Laura ruling the roost as well as these incidents might have given Tom second thoughts. Instead he persuaded Bousie to issue the invitation and bankrolled the renovation of The Ruin.

What were those grownups talking about so earnestly during those summer days on our farm? The dictionary work aside, it seems they were trying to stop the oncoming war, needless to say a failed endeavor. They were enlisted as "insiders," members of Laura's movement for a new world order. People coming to the farm for the day were coming to see if they wanted to join in. I don't know that any did.

Why did Robert Graves and the others show such deference to Laura? They were awed by her brilliant intellect, something I hadn't the foggiest notion about then. They thought she had the answers to the big questions of life; that she would lead them on to good new things. And they were captivated by her strong personality.

Force of personality, Laura had it in capital letters. She was devoted to achieving her own way, and every word she spoke and every action she took was designed to help her in this endeavor.* She could be kind and understanding; she could be untruthful and malevolent. She seemed to have a certain psychic power, which led some to conclude that she had the makings of a witch. In fact her character cannot be truly drawn without reference to her witchly powers, of which there are various instances. I mention one of the last (in 1986) I know of.

Polly Antell, a longtime close friend of Laura's, was curious to meet me and nervously asked me to supper—she knew Laura would strongly disapprove. Immediately after my departure, her phone rang. It was Laura calling, from Florida. "You have just been seeing Griselda," she said, not in the least pleased. Mystified and upset, Polly called Maria, who had arranged the meeting. Had Maria mentioned the arrangement to Laura? No! Then how did Laura know? How did she?

We children felt there was something spooky about Laura. Just recently Kathie told me about her November 1939 birthday when she turned eight. She spent the entire day in dread. Laura was making the cake. How was Kathie to avoid eating it? She was sure it would be poisoned. Something about Laura led to such thoughts. I went to bed at night thinking she might be hiding in my closet, waiting to "get me" if I fell asleep. Something about Laura led me to enlist Ria and try in all seriousness a little voodoo magic. We took our dolls Hannah and Jane and began sticking them with pins. Suddenly we became leery— maybe it would work. So we stopped.

Ma, on the other hand, did not become leery. A self-confi-

---

* I have borrowed this sentence from William Trevor's *Elizabeth Alone*.

dent, straightforward person, certainly never seen as prone to nervous disorders, she was so taken with Laura she did not see that she was in danger and had been ever since Laura first laid eyes on Bousie. Ma never could tell us her version of what had happened in any satisfactory way. The nearest she came was to say once, "I thought Laura was my friend and by the time I realized that she wasn't, it was too late."

And—what did Laura want? She of course wanted her program to move forward—not much seemed to be happening on that score. But what she most fervently wanted was Bousie—wife, four children, Protestant ethic notwithstanding. And early on in the six weeks or so before coming to our farm, Laura began her campaign to secure her heart's desire.

There was Ma, fascinated by the exotic creature that Laura was, and excited—probably overly—by the intellectual goings-on. She was gradually being ostracized from the "insiders," dubbed not only unworthy of being in the group but a source of evil that was hindering its program. And then, there was Ma, her standing threatened by the invasion, indeed the takeover, of her domain, which Laura wasted no time in doing once she arrived on the farm. There were the quick, sharp click-clacks of Laura's footsteps as she blustered around the house, the "Katharine" ringing out—no one else ever called Ma by her full name—the doors closed on endless discussions. Very deliberately Laura pushed Ma to the edge, to a breaking point. And when Ma broke down, Laura, in order to give Bousie a rationale for the sundering of his marriage, equated Ma's mental madness with moral wrong. Ma, she proclaimed, was evil.

And where was Bousie? It seems to me that we hardly saw our beloved Bousie that terrible summer. I think he was actually pretty nutty himself and very much traumatized from seeing Ma in her insanity and trying to deal with it. He swallowed Laura's dictum hook, line, and sinker. What it came down to was that one had to agree that Ma was evil and Laura—and by extension he as well—was good. For years after that time he imposed this dictum on others and together with Laura hurt and even damaged them. He cannot, beloved though he remained, be excused. Maria and I long ago came to the conclusion that if Bousie had ever faced up to the falsity of that dictum, he would have walked straight to the Atlantic Ocean—not far from his Florida home—and never turned back.

There is some puzzle, some mystery, some hard-to-believe about the story of the summer of 1939 that can't be explained without dealing with the unordinary. For while much was as ordinary as can be, something "other" was at work as well. I leave it at that.

AFTERWARDS

Bousie and Laura were together for almost thirty years. They lived in Wabasso, Florida, a place as small as our childhood's Brownsburg. At first they tried to carry on with the dictionary project but they finally gave it up. They kept on working about words, however. One of the results was a posthumous book published not long ago under the title *Rational Meaning*, described by Laura as a "Magna Carta of the human mind." One wonders how any but a devotee will plow through the often tortuous prose.

To augment their slim income, they tried running a citrus-fruit business and for several years packed and shipped baskets and crates of oranges and grapefruits grown without chemical sprays. They got customers through ads in *The New Yorker* and *The Pennsylvania Farmer*. It was not a viable enterprise. Some people who went to Florida to help—among them David Owl and his family—were cast off in a most upsetting manner. In their earlier Florida years Bousie and Laura did a lot of casting off. Their castings-off were traumatic.

Bowing to Bousie, who had come to the conclusion that poetry was not the road to truth telling he had once believed, Laura stopped writing poems and burned whatever she had on a bonfire. She would not give permission for reprints of her collected poems and she published an article in *Chelsea Maga-*

zine in which she pronounced the end of poetry. It could go no farther than the peak she had attained.*

Bousie died on July 4, 1968. Perhaps he didn't need to. The doctors of the Vero Beach hospital were all off playing golf, it seems, and Laura apparently unable to get him any proper medical attention as he lay in the hospital emergency room for hours.

My husband said that the Fourth of July was the appropriate day for Bousie's death since he was such a thoroughly American person/patriot. He had once been a thoroughly enchanting father. The kids and I have not forgotten that.

After Bousie's death Laura used the ensuing years to assure her posthumous reputation. She was kindly and sweet to people who pleased her, vituperative to those who did not. She died in 1991.

Ma outlived them both. When she came home in the spring of 1940, she had a lot on her hands—to start with, upset, alienated children, a broken marriage, and inadequate finances. Having come from a background where there was always the wherewithall to do whatever one wanted as far as cost was concerned, money problems were especially burdensome.

And Ma had the residue of her breakdown to cope with. It was a long time before she was clear of Laura's spell and she had several relapses, of short duration though of course disturbing. But while she had had no weapons with which to withstand Laura's witchly siege, she possessed those that enabled her to win out in the end. Her father had instilled her with sto-

---

* Hardly more than two years after Bousie's death, she authorized a book of her selected poems.

icism—if you fall down, get right up again and keep on going. And that Ma did. She was undaunted and uncomplaining and met the challenges as they came along, were they learning how to cook or how to earn a living. And she approached life with interest and enthusiasm. For years she never said a derogatory word about Laura. That used to bother me; it somehow seemed unhealthy. But I came to realize it was a protective stance and only when she felt no longer threatened would Ma say anything negative about Laura. It is interesting to note that once the time came when Ma was completely recovered, our theretofore agnostic mother joined the Catholic Church and for the better part of thirty years rarely missed a daily mass.

Ma's first earning-a-living venture was a woolens shop in New Hope. How she dealt with the garment district of New York City is a mystery. But she did manage to get consignments of fine fabrics, line up tailors to custom-make suits and coats, and for several years tried to turn a profit. Failing that, Ma went to work for the Japanese-American architect and furniture designer and maker George Nakashima. She worked with sandpaper and tungseed oil and learned several four-letter words from her co-workers. After that she took a job in Greenwich, Connecticut acting as surrogate mother for two orphaned teenagers, niece and nephew of one of her boarding school friends. Next she served as a housemother at Lesley College in Cambridge, Massachusetts, where she audited courses at Harvard. In the late 1960's she settled in Brunswick, Maine, sharing a house with Maria. She took a Red Cross nurses aide course and despite having been told she was too old, graduated at the top of the class. She then had a number of assignments helping housebound elderly people. Until a few months before she died Ma gardened, took brisk walks—in the winter skied, practiced the recorder, knitted countless hats, vests, socks, studied Spanish, flew kites and read a great many books.

In the long run of her life—she was nearly ninety-four when she died in 1995—Ma triumphed in ways both large and small and held the admiration and deep affection of many.

AS FOR ME . . .

As for me, being twelve years old in the summer of 1939, I had already had a full run of untroubled childhood, something "my kids"—Maria, Kathie, and Ben—variously missed out on. Gradually I stopped thinking of them as "the kids." We all, as the saying goes, grew up, each to have her or his own life story yet forever marked by the *Once*—both the good and bad of it—that we shared long ago.

The sailing was difficult at times during my teens and twenties but life is full of surprises. One wonderful surprise (mentioned in the *Jackson Quarterly* news) was the arrival out of the blue in late August, just when there was very little wind in my sails, of a radio, a battery-operated Emerson. This was sent to me by Mrs. Lincoln, one of Ma's lifelong boarding-school friends. The thoughtfulness behind it moves me still. This radio, a fake-tweed covered box sitting on my bedroom windowsill, was a companion taking me away from the happenings of the past few months and introducing me to Jack Benny, Helen Hayes, Kate Smith and her "God Bless America," the Shadow, Helen Trent and matinee idol Gil, Fibber McGee, the Grand Ol' Opry, Mr. Kaltenborn and the news. And I didn't need to miss an episode of the *Lone Ranger* show. It is not too much to say that the radio was a key element in the wind coming back into my sails.

And then a few years later, another unforgettable surprise came my way, Things had just settled down after a particularly upset period. I was at my job and opening the day's mail. Here, was an envelope addressed to me. From the Cunard Lines. The contents:

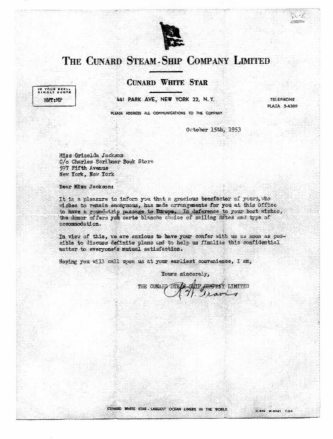

The Lake District, Southey's grandson, and so much more— here I come! The Generous Benefactor, forever undiscovered.

About the Author

GRISELDA JACKSON OHANNESSIAN was born in New York City in 1927. After studying literature and music at Columbia University, she joined New Directions in 1956. During her lifelong tenure at the press, Mrs. Ohannessian worked in almost every department—editorial, publicity, and production. In 1983, she was appointed Vice President by James Laughlin, New Directions' founder and publisher, becoming President upon his death in 1997. Although she retired in 2005, she remains a Trustee of the New Directions Ownership Trust and a member of the New Directions Board. Mrs. Ohannessian has three daughters, Ani, Lucy, and Mary, and four grand-children. She lives in New York City.